Gross error p. 104 Use in exam!

p. 114
119
,50
151 ?

A Technical Services Manual for Small Libraries

by

John B. Corbin

The Scarecrow Press, Inc.
Metuchen, N. J.   1971

Contents

INTRODUCTION

This manual has been written for the practicing librarian in a small- to medium-sized library (college, school, public, or special) who suddenly has thrust upon him the responsibility of organizing and/or administering a technical services department. By no means is it expected to be a substitute for good formal courses in a library school; rather it is designed to serve as a refresher to those who have forgotten their formal training and as an aid to those who are partially trained.

This manual must be used in conjunction with the standard texts already available on technical services work. It should aid the librarian in organizing his routines and procedures; guide him through the exacting processes of acquisitions work, cataloging and classification, and further processing of materials for use; and lead him to further references and readings that will provide more detailed information and further knowledge on the work involved.

It is based on ten years of work experience in a variety of technical services departments and on two manuals previously published by the Texas State Library: A Technical Processing Manual for Small Public Libraries: Cataloging (Monograph no. 1, 1962) and A Technical Services Manual for Small Libraries (Monograph no. 3, 1965).

While many people rightfully should be thanked for encouragement to the author (including the staff of the Scarecrow Press), the help of two special people in my life must

be awarded grateful appreciation: Miss Mary Pound, Chief
Catalog Librarian, The University of Texas at Austin,
Austin, Texas, for her encouragement and faith, and Mr.
Ralph Funk, Director, Oklahoma Department of Libraries,
Oklahoma City, Oklahoma, for being himself.

JBC

ORGANIZATION OF THE TECHNICAL SERVICES DEPARTMENT

The technical services department is one of the most complex, the least understood, yet one of the most vital units of a library's organizational structure. This department, whose efforts and products affect practically every service offered by other units of the library, is a key element in the difference between a library giving excellent service to its public and one giving inadequate or mediocre service. However well a library's collection or collections are selected, displayed, or utilized ...

> if there are delays in ordering and receiving materials,
>
> if there are delays in cataloging and classifying materials,
>
> if there are delays in the further processing of materials,
>
> if the processing is shoddy and haphazard,
>
> if the index files and other records are poorly organized, prepared, and maintained,

then the effectiveness of other departments such as reference and circulation will be reduced proportionately.

In short, a library's services to its public are dependent to a large extent upon the quality and quantity of work and the efficiency of its technical services department.

In order to provide superior yet inexpensive and rapid service, a technical services department must be well organized and managed; adequately staffed, housed, and equipped; and goal-oriented towards quality and dependable service.

To this end, this department must have an open and
well-used channel of constructive communication with every
other department of the library. Since the technical services
department normally has little direct contact with the public,
its administrator and other staff members must be responsive
to the needs of other units of the library that do provide
daily and equally vital services direct to library users.
These staff members are in a position to know what the public needs or is demanding.

Functions and Organization of Technical Services

The term "technical services," which variously is
referred to as "technical processing," "processing,"
"preparations," or even an organizationally-separate "acquisitions" or "ordering" and "cataloging," is relatively new.
According to Maurice Tauber, it came into being

> ... to decrease the span of control of the head
> librarian; to accelerate the flow of processed
> materials; to reduce the cost of preparing materials
> for use; and to develop among the various depart-
> ments a spirit of cooperation. [1]

The technical services department of a library is that
unit which traditionally is charged with the functions of:

1. Ordering and receiving materials for the
   library's collection or collections;

2. Organizing, cataloging, and classifying these
   materials;

3. Organizing, preparing, and maintaining all
   necessary catalogs, records, and files for the
   collection or collections;

4. Pasting, labelling, stamping, and further preparing the materials for use.

Allied functions sometimes assigned to this department are

the binding or preparation for binding of materials; the mending or repairing of materials; and the inventorying of the collection or collections.

Tauber further states that:

> Such factors as tradition, personnel, physical quarters, financial support, types and distribution of collections, and the personalities, qualifications, and attitudes of administrative officers and staff have accounted for variations in organization.[2]

While variations in organization will exist, a typical functional organizational chart for a small- to medium-sized library is shown in Figure 1.

Staffing of Technical Services

In a small library, whether it be public, college, school, or special, one of the most important influences upon its organization will be the size of its staff.

The organizational chart in Figure 1 is one of function or services provided and does not necessarily reflect the number of persons on the staff. In a very small library, one person might have to serve simultaneously as the head librarian, the public services librarian, and the technical services librarian! In this case, this person simply must allocate his time and efforts among the different responsibilities as he sees fit or as time allows.

More typical would be a situation in which one person serves as the head librarian, one as the public services librarian, and another as the technical services librarian. In a larger library, these people would have one or more additional staff members aiding them in performing their assigned functions.

There are many possibilities for distributing duties among staff members in a technical services department; the

number of staff available, the services to be performed, the
experience of the administrator, and even the space and
equipment available to the department will exert influences on
these assignments. For example, the technical services department might have one person assigned to order and
receive materials; one to catalog and classify the materials;
one to type and file; and another to paste, label, and perform
miscellaneous duties.

The larger the library, the greater the need for a
distinct and separate allocation of duties between the various
staff members; otherwise, a serious overlapping of duties
and a resulting loss of efficiency of services could occur.

An organizational chart for a typical technical services
department of a small- to medium-sized library, indicating
functions and personnel assigned to perform those functions
is shown in Figure 2.

Only a large library can afford to have a person whose
sole duties are the administration of the technical services
department and the supervision of its personnel. However,
even in the small library, one person alone must have the
responsibility and authority to plan, organize, and supervise
the department's activities and to be a spokesman for the
unit to the head librarian and to other departments of the
library. These administrative and supervisory duties might
have to be performed along with other day-to-day work such
as cataloging and classification but, nonetheless, a responsible, strong, and single voice is mandatory for the efficient
operation of a technical services department.

Again recognizing that the size of a library and funds
available to it will dictate the quantity and quality of its
staff, at least one librarian should be assigned to the technical services department if at all possible. The areas of

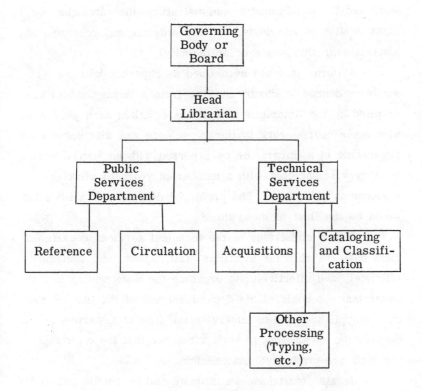

Figure 1.--A simplified functional organizational chart for a small- to medium-sized library

responsibility in technical services most needing professional work are the department's administration, the cataloging and classification of materials, and the ordering and receiving of materials (in this sequence or priority).

A librarian could be defined as a person with a master's degree in library science from a library school accredited by the American Library Association; as a person with some course work in library science and with some work experience in a library; or as a person with no course work in library science but with a number of years of work experience in a library. The preferred definition of a librarian would be the first of these three.

The administrator of the technical services department must have the abilities to utilize staff, space, and equipment efficiently and effectively; to organize the work wisely in order that the goals of the department and of the library can be accomplished; and to supervise the flow of materials through the department in such a manner that the efforts of the staff are productive and efficient.

He also must have an intimate and pragmatic knowledge of all phases of technical services work and an understanding of their relationships to one another. Above all, the administrator must have that elusive spark of enthusiasm and zeal for his work that catches and focuses the inspiration of his staff and creates a desire in them to work with and for him.

The ordering and receiving of materials, typing, filing, pasting, labelling, and so on can be assigned to library assistants and clerks if these people are carefully selected, adequately trained, and properly supervised.

A library assistant could be defined as a person with a bachelor's degree and possibly with some course work in

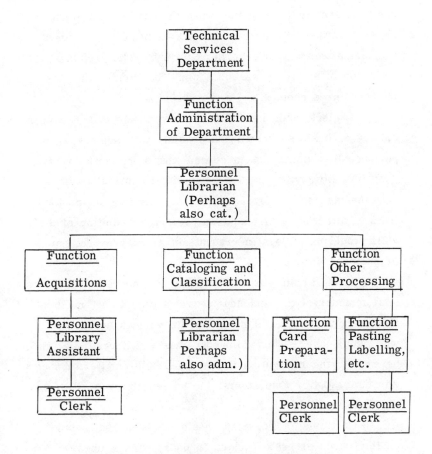

Figure 2.--A simplified organizational chart for
a typical technical services department of a
small- to medium-sized library indicating function
and personnel assigned to perform these functions.

library science; as a person with some course work in library science and with some work experience in a library; or as a person with no course work in library science but with some work experience in a library. The preferred definition of a library assistant would be, again, the first of these three choices.

A clerk could be defined as a graduate of a two-year college or business school and possibly with some work experience in a library; as a person with some work experience in a library; or as a person with no formal training past the high school level but who will receive on-the-job training after he is hired. The preferred definition of a clerk would be at least a graduate of a two-year college or business school.

In the small library flexibility is important, and each staff member of the technical services department must be able to perform most if not all of its various operations with equal ease. This philosophy must, of course, be tempered with the realization that some people can perform certain duties better than others; the administrator must recognize talent and use it to its best advantages.

Certainly, a librarian should not be asked to type catalog cards or paste pockets in books, and a library assistant or clerk should not be expected to catalog and classify materials without proper training. Nonetheless, people are absent from work at times and work does accumulate for various reasons during peak periods of activity and often due to unforeseen circumstances.

A temporary shifting of personnel from their normal duties to bottleneck areas can assure an even flow of materials through the department at all times; this flexibility usually will indicate the difference between a superior department and a mediocre one.

Quarters for Technical Services

The major factors influencing the design of quarters for technical services will be:

1. The size of the department's staff
2. The functions assigned to the department
3. The funds available to the library for technical services
4. The space available for technical services

If a building is being renovated, the physical arrangement or shape and size of the existing building will influence the quarters available for technical services. If a new building is being constructed, the chances are greater that ideal quarters suited for the technical services functions can be designed and constructed.

The few standards available to the administrator for designing quarters for technical services are generally vague and not of much value; the estimated space requirements vary from 100 to 150 square feet per staff member. However, there are some rule-of-thumb "standards" or desired characteristics for the quarters of an adequate technical services department. The main considerations for planning quarters for the department are:

1. The department's location in relationship to other departments of the library;
2. Its physical size, shape, and flexibility of design;
3. The relationships of work areas within the department;
4. Its location in relationship to shipping and receiving facilities;

5. Its environmental comfort in regard to heat-
    ing, cooling, lighting, etc.

Location in Relationship to Other Departments of the
Library. --While it is true that the technical services department can be separated or isolated from other departments
of the library without a major loss of service to the public,
this idea should be discouraged.

As an organizer, preparer, and maintainer of the
card catalog, the technical services department should be
quartered as near as possible to this index or have easy
and ready access to it. Since the shelf list of the collection or collections normally is housed in the technical services department, this file should be readily available to the
staffs of the reference and circulation departments, who
have many occasions to use it.

The technical services department is the prime user
of ordering, cataloging, and classification aids; but, again,
the reference and circulation departments and sometimes
even the public need to use these materials.

For these reasons, if for no other, the technical
services department should be close to the reference and
circulation areas of the library, preferably on the same
floor. If not on the same floor, then the department should
have close access to an elevator or to nearby stairs leading
to the public areas of the library.

Another reason, which is often overlooked or ignored,
for having the technical services department near the public
services departments is entirely a psychological one. Any
department separated from other units of the library by
space or by physical barriers tends to lose some of its
feeling of identity or relationship with the organization as
a whole, unless the head librarian is very careful to

minimize these disadvantages by establishing good lines of
communication between the department heads and to empha-
size the interdependence of all departments and their staffs.

Physical Size, Shape, and Flexibility of Design. --If
the designer of a technical services department has his
choice, he should require a square or rectangular room
with no permanent obstructions or walls, with the possible
exception of required pillars or columns. This will allow
flexibility in arranging furniture, equipment, and staff within
the area.

By placing free-standing shelving, filing cabinets, or
other pieces of equipment in different arrangements, a
sense of privacy can be maintained for the staff, and noise
can be reduced or minimized.

Private offices for the administrator and/or catalog-
er(s) might be desirable, preferably with glass being used
extensively for the major part of the offices' walls.

Relationships of Work Areas Within the Department. --
There are certain operations within a technical services department which logically should be placed close or adjacent
to each other. Since the department's efficiency depends to
a great extent upon assembly line techniques, the work areas
should be so arranged that work can flow easily and evenly
through the areas without doubling back upon itself.

For example, staff members in both the acquisitions
section and the cataloging and classification section will use
the bibliographic and verification aids. Therefore, these
tools should be close at hand to both these work areas, if
not between them. The "on order" and "in process" files
probably will be used by the cataloger and by the order
clerk and should be easily accessible to both.

The person who prepares catalog and shelf list cards will work closely with the cataloger, so their work areas should be close together (but not too close, because of the noise of the typewriters and/or other equipment which may disrupt the cataloger's work).

Pasting, labelling, placing plastic jackets on books, and other final preparation steps for materials are of similar nature and should be clustered together, but they do not necessarily have to be near the areas where the functions of acquisitions, cataloging and classification, and preparation of cards are performed.

As indicated in Figure 2, there are three main "clusters" of activities within technical services: acquisitions, cataloging and classification, and other processing.

In order to visualize easily this flow of work through the department, the librarian should imagine, for example, unprocessed materials arriving through a front door and being unpacked and placed on a book truck; the truck rolling down the length of the department having various operations performed on the materials on the way (receiving and invoicing, cataloging and classification, card preparation, pasting, labelling, etc.); then the material rolling out the back door on the same truck completely processed and ready for use by the public.

A graphic and highly-simplified representation of some suggested relationships of work areas is shown in Figure 3. Since the possible combinations for locating desks, files, shelving, and other equipment is endless and dependent almost entirely upon local conditions, no attempt has been made to suggest their arrangement within the areas. Some common-sense thinking and a few sketches on paper made by the administrator in consultation with his staff can result in a good arrangement of equipment within the work areas.

Location in Relationship to Shipping and Receiving Facilities. --A technical services department needs easy access to shipping and receiving areas. If such space cannot be incorporated physically into its quarters, then the department should be adjacent to such facilities. Since the shipping and receiving of materials, supplies, and equipment usually is a noisy affair and requires the frequent opening and closing of outside doors, a separate area from the main work areas of technical services would be desirable, with weather- and sound-proof doors between.

Environmental Comfort. --The need for proper acoustic controls, adequate lighting (natural lighting, if possible), heating, cooling, tile or carpet floor-covering, bright and cheerful colors, water fountains, lounge facilities, and so on are as essential to a technical services department as they are to the reference or circulation departments or to the head librarian.

Equipment and Supplies for Technical Services

Just as the technical services department has a valid need and a right to adequate environmental comfort, so it has the right and need for good equipment. Cast-off, beat-up, and shoddy furniture and equipment have as little place in a technical services department as they do in any public services department of the library.

In addition to the desks, chairs, filing cabinets, typing tables, typewriters, and the usual equipment found in most other parts of the library, the technical services

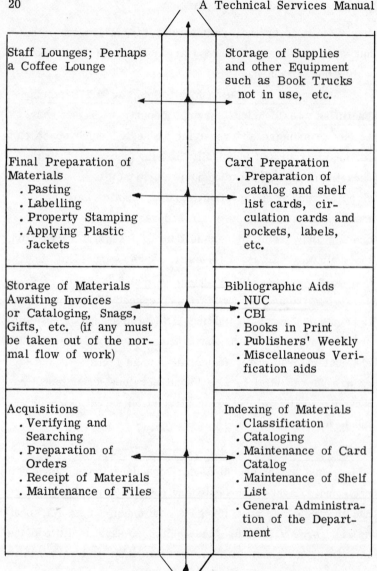

Staff Lounges; Perhaps a Coffee Lounge	Storage of Supplies and other Equipment such as Book Trucks not in use, etc.
Final Preparation of Materials . Pasting . Labelling . Property Stamping . Applying Plastic Jackets	Card Preparation . Preparation of catalog and shelf list cards, circulation cards and pockets, labels, etc.
Storage of Materials Awaiting Invoices or Cataloging, Snags, Gifts, etc. (if any must be taken out of the normal flow of work)	Bibliographic Aids . NUC . CBI . Books in Print . Publishers' Weekly . Miscellaneous Verification aids
Acquisitions . Verifying and Searching . Preparation of Orders . Receipt of Materials . Maintenance of Files	Indexing of Materials . Classification . Cataloging . Maintenance of Card Catalog . Maintenance of Shelf List . General Administration of the Department

Figure 3. --A suggested arrangement of work areas
within a technical services department (areas
shown are not necessarily drawn to
actual proportions)

department has a need for some special furniture and equipment.

Catalog card cabinets are needed for the "on order" and "in process" files, the shelf list or lists, and other authority files; shelving is needed for the storage of materials awaiting processing and for the bibliographic aids (including perhaps a special cabinet for the Cumulative Book Index volumes); and large work tables are necessary for using the bibliographic aids, for pasting, labelling, and placing plastic jackets on books.

Special equipment necessary for technical services work could be an adding machine and perhaps a billing or posting machine to be used in ordering and receiving materials; electric erasers used in the preparation of catalog and shelf list cards; an office copier for copying invoices, letters, or even catalog cards; and pasting and labelling devices used to speed up those processes.

Special supplies essential to technical services work include catalog card stock, guide cards for the catalogs and shelf lists, paste or glue, spine labels, plastic jackets, rubber property stamps, in addition to supplies such as paper, pencils, paper clips, etc., common to other departments of the library.

Notes

1. Maurice F. Tauber and Associates, Technical Services in Libraries: Acquisitions, Cataloging, Classification (New York: Columbia University Press, 1953), p. 10.

2. Ibid., p. 9.

SELECTION OF MATERIALS

Types of Materials in a Library

Materials to be found in the collection or collections of a library can include books, pamphlets, periodicals, newspapers, manuscripts, paintings, pictures, clippings, maps, music scores, motion picture films, filmstrips, slides, phonodisc recordings, tapes, such micro-reproductions as microfilm, microprint, microfiche, and so on.

While most small libraries will have only books, pamphlets, periodicals, and newspapers in their collections, other types of materials should be added if the need is apparent and if adequate funds, staff, and space are available.

Domestic In-Print Books. --Broadly interpreted, a domestic in-print book can be defined as any book, regardless of its language or origin of publication, which is in-stock and available from a publisher, distributor, or reprinter in the United States. The traditional definition is any book published in the United States and currently available from its original publisher or distributor.

Domestic Out-of-Print Books. --If a book is no longer available from its original publisher or distributor, from a reprinter, from a jobber, or through the usual book store, then the item is considered to be "out-of-print."

Pamphlets. --There is no common agreement as to the definition of a pamphlet; most librarians adopt their own definition and may or may not follow it in actual practice. A pamphlet is defined in the A. L. A. Glossary of Library Terms as:

22

> ... an independent publication consisting of a few
> leaves of printed matter stitched together but not
> bound; usually enclosed in paper covers ... there
> is variation in the maximum number of leaves or
> pages allowed under the term. For the purposes
> of statistics and method, some librarians set the
> limit at 80 pages ...; others consider 'about 100
> pages' sufficient restriction ... [1]

Most librarians will not categorize an item as a pamphlet until it has been received and examined. Others
rightly are not concerned about the size of an item but
judge its estimated short- or long-range value to the library.

Periodicals. --A periodical is:

> A publication with a distinctive title intended to
> appear in successive (usually unbound) numbers
> or parts at stated or regular intervals and, as a
> rule, for an indefinite time. Each part generally
> contains articles by several contributors ... [2]

The frequency of publication of parts or issues of a
periodical ranges from weekly, monthly, bi-monthly, quarterly, and so on, to an infrequent publication schedule.
Most librarians require that more than one issue of an item
be published during a year before it is considered a periodical. Publications issued daily are commonly referred to as
newspapers rather than as periodicals.

The word "periodical" is often used interchangeably
with "magazine."

Newspapers. --A newspaper is:

> A publication issued at stated and frequent inter-
> vals, usually daily, weekly, or semiweekly, which
> reports events and discusses topics of current
> interest. [3]

Nonbook Materials. --The recent trend toward and
widely-accepted dependence upon more and more "nonbook,"
"audio-visual," or "newer media" materials has placed much

pressure on libraries to acquire, organize, and make available to users such materials as motion picture films, filmstrips, slides, phonodisc recordings, tapes, microfilms,
microprint, microfiche, music scores, and other "multi-
media" kits containing one or more of the items listed
above (and sometimes also a book or books). Even framed
pictures, which can be circulated in a manner similar to
books, are becoming a part of the permanent collections of
many libraries.

    Foreign Materials. --The term "foreign material"
will be used in this manual to designate any item published
outside the United States, including those published in the
English language and those published in other languages.
It should be noted here, however, that many titles in languages other than English are published routinely by domestic
publishers (that is, within the United States). These titles
can be acquired in the same manner as are other domestic
in-print books.

The Selection Process

    The process of choosing or selecting books and other
materials precedes all acquisitions or order work. Requests
for the purchase of materials for the library's collection or
collections can originate either from the library's staff or
from the library's users. In a college library, for example,
a large portion of the requests should be made by the
school's teaching faculty.

    The type of library; the nature and needs of its clien-
tele; the adequacy or inadequacy of the library's present
collection or collections; the size of its budget for the purchase of materials; the estimated worth of items requested
for purchase; and even the library's proximity to another

library acquiring the same types of materials--all of these contribute to the selection decisions.

This manual is concerned primarily with the tech-niques or organization of technical services work, and no attempt except this cursory one to cover the selection of materials will be made; however, a bibliography of readings on the topic is included at the end of this manual.

Most libraries will have some sort of screening pro-cess for requests for purchase of library materials some-where in the system before the technical services depart-ment can begin its work.

For example, the library should have a policy that all requests for purchase be funnelled through one person (the head librarian, for example) for approval or disapproval before they are forwarded to technical services for ordering. In a college library, the chairman of each teaching depart-ment should require that all requests for the purchase of materials to be placed in the library be approved by him before they are forwarded to the library.

Preparation of Order Cards

The person selecting materials should complete a 3-by-5-inch slip or card (commonly known as an "order card" and hereby called such) for each item requested, suggested, or noted for possible purchase. Order cards for replacement copies or needed duplicates can be added to this file also.

The following information is the suggested minimum necessary on an order card:

1. Author's surname and given names or initials;
2. Title of book or other materials;
3. Edition number, if other than the first;

4.   Publisher's name;

5.   Copyright date or date of publication, if
     known;

6.   Number of copies wanted;

7.   List price (price before discount) per copy,
     if known;

8.   The name of the person requesting the materi-
     al, the fund or department to which the request
     is to be charged, or both; for example, "John
     Smith, Reference Department"; "Dr. Jones,
     Chemistry Department"; etc.

Another item which might be of value in the ordering
process is the requestor's source of information for selecting the material; for example, "Booklist, December 19XX,
p. 29"; "Choice, May 19XX, p. 101"; etc. If an item was
selected after receipt of a brochure or flyer from the publisher, this announcement also can be forwarded with the
request for purchase.

Order cards also can be prepared for materials
other than books. Notation should be made on the cards as
to the medium of the material if other than a book (pamphlet, periodical, microfilm, map, etc.) in order that possible purchasing errors and delays can be avoided.

These order cards, with the authors' surnames at
the top, should be alphabetized for easy handling. As new
cards are added, these can be interfiled, or, if a decision
is reached not to purchase particular items, the order
cards can be withdrawn. Separate files for different types
of materials can be maintained if this is considered necessary.

When the final selection of materials has been made
and all have been screened and approved for purchase (if
this is the policy of the library), the order cards are forwarded to the technical services department for ordering.

A variety of stock order cards can be purchased from most library supply houses, or almost any printing firm can custom-print order cards to suit the library's particular needs. A point to keep in mind when purchasing stock order cards or in preparing specifications for custom-printed cards will be the intended use of the cards and the extent of that use.

For example, if the order card is to be used throughout the requesting, verifying, searching, and ordering procedures, filed for a period of time in the "on order" file and later in the "in process" file, then a good quality of paper or card stock should be selected to insure that the card will not wear out before its usefulness is ended.

Also, special spaces might be needed for the addition of (for example) discount prices, call numbers, subject headings, dates of receipt, and so on, gathered as the material progresses through the various stages of processing, if the order card is used in this manner.

Class No.	Author (surname first) Ricard, Matthieu			
Accession No.	Title Mystery of animal migration			
No. of copies ordered 1				
Date ordered	Publisher and Place Hill and Wang			Year 1969
Dealer	Edition or series	Volumes	List Price $5.95	Cost
Date received	Requested by Davis		Notify Davis	
Date of bill	Reviewed in Booklist, Dec.1, 19XX			General
L. C. card No.	Approved by RBD			Fund Charged
GAYLORD 101-L				PRINTED IN U.S.A.

Figure 4. --An order card ready to be forwarded to technical services for ordering

On the other hand, if the order card is to serve
only until the information on the card is transferred to a
multiple-copy order form, then the quality of the paper or
card stock for the order card is inconsequential and spaces
for a minimum amount of information should be reserved.

Figure 4 is an order card ready to be forwarded to
the technical services.

Notes

1. American Library Association. Committee on Library
    Terminology, A. L. A. Glossary of Library Terms,
    With a Selection of Terms in Related Fields, ed. by
    Elizabeth H. Thompson (Chicago: American Library
    Association, 1943), pp. 96-97.

2. Ibid. , p. 99.

3. Ibid, p. 91.

ACQUISITION OF MATERIALS

"Acquisitions work in a library is the means by which additions are made to the library's collection."[1] This work usually includes the ordering and receiving of all types of materials and maintaining of any records (copies of purchase orders, invoices, "on order" and "in process" files, correspondence, etc.) necessary for these additions.

Verifying and Searching Information for Requests for Purchase

Verifying and searching information for requests for purchase becomes increasingly necessary as a library's collection or collections and book budget grow. These procedures include correcting misspelled words or names, adding to or deleting from the given information, and verifying the availability and cost of the material. While the persons selecting materials do not intentionally give incorrect or imprecise or incomplete information, the fact is that they often do supply inaccurate information.

Two important reasons for verifying information on requests for purchase before purchase orders are prepared are:

1. To eliminate or minimize the possibility of ordering unwanted duplicate copies of materials;

2. To reduce or minimize delays in receiving ordered materials by giving the vendor correct bibliographic information initially.

29

For example, the author's name on an order card, as copied from a selection aid, might be "Twain, Mark," while Twain's real name, "Clemens, Samuel Langhorne," might be used in the library's card catalog. Thus, without the verification procedures, a new order might be placed for a title which is already in the library's collection.

Or, if a book should be ordered without verification as The Cloak of the West, when the correct title actually is A History of Badmen; the Code of the West, a vendor might not be able to obtain the correct title at all, or at least not without long delays and much correspondence with the library and/or the publisher.

Verification of information consists of comparing the information given on an order card submitted as a request for purchase with the information in certain standard bibliographic aids which the librarian considers as "authorities," and of changing, deleting, or adding information when necessary.

The extent of verification of information will depend upon the intended use of that information. If information on the order card is to be used solely to prepare an order, then little beyond the spelling and correctness of the author and title and the availability and cost from a publisher or vendor should be verified.

If printed cards are to be purchased and used later in the cataloging and classification phases of processing, some additional information must be located and recorded (see pages 100ff for a further description of printed cards). If printed cards are not to be used or cannot be obtained for particular titles, then the more information located and recorded initially during the verification phase and the more

correct and reliable that information is, the easier the work
of the cataloger will be after the material is received.

When the verification of information on requests for
purchase has been completed, one additional step is necessary
before a purchase order can be prepared. The order cards
for those items to be ordered should be arranged by author
(or main entry) and searched in the card catalog to make
certain that the new requests are not already in the library's
collection or collections; in the "on order" file to make certain that they are not on order but unreceived; and in the
"in process" file to make certain that they have not been
ordered, received, and are currently being processed for
the shelves.

If the library's collection or collections and files
are small and the librarian knows the material in them
well, these searches might not be necessary; but unwanted
duplicate copies are a waste of time and, more importantly,
money.

Figure 5 is the order card shown in Figure 4 after
it has been verified, searched, and considered ready to be
placed on order.

Below are listed some common bibliographic aids
for verifying requests for purchase of different types of materials in a small- or medium-sized library. Complete
citations and a brief annotation of each are located at the
end of this manual.

Domestic Books. --Some widely-accepted bibliographic
aids for verifying information on requests for purchase of
domestic books (both in-print and out-of-print) are the
National Union Catalog, the Publishers' Weekly, the American Book Publishing Record, the Cumulative Book Index,

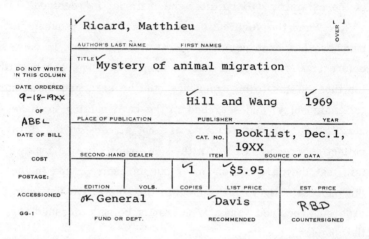

Figure 5.--An order card for a request for purchase
which has been verified and searched and is ready to
be included on a purchase order

and the titles within the Standard Catalog Series of the H. W.
Wilson Company (Children's Catalog, Junior High School Li-
brary Catalog, Senior High School Library Catalog, Fiction
Catalog, and Public Library Catalog).

If the library owns a copy of the latest edition of
Books in Print (and it should!), time will be saved by locating
requests for purchase in this aid to obtain the latest correct
price and publisher of each before preparing an order. A
trade book not listed here will usually be out-or-print; however, as some publishers do not have any of their titles
listed in Books in Print, some may not be listed but will be
in-print and available. Books published since the last edition
of Books in Print might not be included here either. Conversely, some titles listed in Books in Print will become out-
of-print between the annual editions of this aid.

If the librarian can't determine whether an item is in-print or not, a query to the publisher can be made. Figure 6 is a form letter which can be used for this purpose.

Prices also can be found in some of the other bibliographic aids listed above - even lately the National Union Catalog; but Books in Print is considered to be the most reliable aid because it is a quick index to recent lists of books for sale as given by the publisher themselves.

Pamphlets. -- Locating bibliographic information for pamphlets can be more difficult than for books, depending upon the size (in pages) of the pamphlet, the importance or currency of the subject or subjects covered in the publication, and often simply the importance of the publisher or his means of publicizing and distributing his publications.

Prices, publishers, and other bibliographic information for pamphlets can be found in the Vertical File Index and often in the standard aids listed above for verifying domestic in-print books. As a rule, pamphlets are not listed in the Books in Print, though some can be found there. Pamphlets are excluded from the Cumulative Book Index and generally from the Standard Catalog Series of the H. W. Wilson Company.

If pamphlets are not cataloged by the library but are simply placed in a pamphlet or vertical file, requests for the more expensive pamphlets should be checked in that file to avoid duplication. Due to the small cost of most pamphlets, occasional duplication of some titles is not a major mistake.

The form letter in Figure 6 can be used to inquire about prices or the availability of pamphlets, if these are unknown.

Anytown Public Library
123 Bay Street
Zero, Texas 78711

Gentlemen:

The Library would like to acquire the item(s) listed
below:

Would you please quote a price for any or all of these
that are available from you?   This is not an order but
a request for information.

Sincerely,

John B. Corbin
Librarian

Figure 6. --A form letter used to determine the
availability of a variety of types of materials

Periodicals. --Verifying and searching information
for requests for periodical subscriptions before the orders
are placed is not as important as for book requests; the
chance of ordering unwanted duplicate subscriptions is relatively low in a small library. However, a list of new subscriptions should be compared with the list of old subscriptions to avoid possible unintentional duplication.

The three most important items to be verified for a
periodical subscription are:

1. The correct and latest title of the periodical;

2. The publisher of the periodical;

3. Whether the periodical is being published
currently and the cost of an annual, biennial,
etc. , subscription.

If there is more than one periodical with the same title, then the publisher and/or place of publication will be important in identifying the particular title wanted.

Prices, publishers, and other bibliographic information for most periodicals purchased by the small library can be found in the latest editions of Ayer's Directory of Newspapers, Magazines, and Trade Publications or Ulrich's International Periodicals Directory. Also, most periodical subscription agents publish lists of the titles which they handle; these lists will include sufficient information to allow orders to be placed.

Newspapers. --The four most important items to be verified for a newspaper subscription are:

1. The correct and latest title of the newspaper;

2. The publisher's name and address;

3. Whether the newspaper is currently being published;

4. The cost of an annual, biennial, etc., subscription.

Prices, publishers, and other bibliographic information for newspapers can be found also in the latest edition of Ayer's Directory of Newspapers, Magazines, and Trade Publications.

Nonbook Materials. --For most nonbook materials, little verification or searching can be done before ordering. If a library's collection of materials in a particular medium (in microfilm, for example) is extensive, a check of the files should be made to avoid duplication by a new order.

Foreign Materials. --The most common bibliographic aid available in the United States for verifying titles published outside the United States in English and in foreign languages is the National Union Catalog. Foreign titles

published or distributed simultaneously in the United States
are listed often in the Publishers' Weekly and the American
Book Publishing Record.

Methods of Acquiring Materials

Three common methods of acquiring materials for a
library are by purchase, by gift, and by exchange.

Purchase. --Monies appropriated to a library from
municipal, county, regional, state, or federal funds, gifts
of money, endowments, collections of money from book
fines, book sales, book rentals, and so on, are the bases
of purchases.

While materials normally are acquired by initially
sending purchase orders prepared from the verified and
searched order cards to publishers or to a jobber, there
are two other indirect methods: by "standing order" and
by "blanket order. "

In the case of many types of publications (such as
annuals or yearbooks, supplements to other titles, or mul-
tiple-volumed sets when publication of the individual volumes
or parts will be spread over several years), many libraries
use a "standing order" arrangement with publishers or their
jobber to have each new title, part, volume, and so on,
shipped automatically as published. This also is referred
to as a "continuation order. "

Examples of materials which can be placed on a
standing order basis with their publishers or with a jobber
are such titles as Information Please Almanac; World Book
Yearbook; Annual Review of ... ; Yearbook of ... ; or perhaps the Collected Works of ..., in cases where one or two
volumes of the set are to be published each year and the set
will not be completed for many years to come.

Another type of standing order is a request to a publisher or jobber that all future titles to be published in a particular series be shipped automatically when issued. For example, if the library wishes to acquire all future titles to be published in the "Pictorial Histories of the Presidents" series, this series can be placed on a standing order basis.

The other method of acquiring materials similar to a standing order is referred to as a "blanket order." In this case, certain subject areas are specified by the librarian and the publisher or jobber will ship automatically each new title that is published on the subject or subjects chosen.

Blanket orders can be beneficial to very large libraries with sizeable book budgets since they would normally be purchasing virtually every new title published in certain subject areas each year in any case. Few small libraries can justify the blanket order method of acquiring materials, mainly because their book budgets are extremely limited and each new title purchased must be carefully selected in order to obtain the very best for their library users.

While the library will have the right to return any unsuitable title received on a blanket order, the danger to the small library lies in the fact that titles of questionable or borderline value, once received, are easier to keep than to return to the vendor for credit. Funds can be spent to greater advantage on titles selected individually and of known value.

The small library, nevertheless, can use the blanket order method of acquiring materials to great advantage if it is approached cautiously and in a limited manner. For example, if the library has a local history collection, a blanket order could be placed for all books written about or by an author in the particular region in which the library is

located. This would reduce the number of titles acquired
annually in this manner to a small number, which probably
would be well within the limits of the library's budget.

As it is difficult to determine exactly when new annuals or yearbooks, supplements, new volumes of a set,
new titles in a series, or books on specific subjects are
to be published, standing or blanket order arrangements with
publishers or a jobber are efficient methods of obtaining
such titles.

Another advantage of a standing or blanket order arrangement is that the publications usually can be obtained
before or shortly after the actual date of publication; thus
the library's users can benefit by having information available rapidly.

Gifts. --Many libraries depend heavily on gifts of material for their collections. The sources of gifts can be
wide and varied, depending upon the public relations pro-
gram of the library and its image in the community, its
policies and procedures, and its imagination. Possible
donors are individuals; civic and professional organizations,
clubs, and groups; foundations; business and industrial
firms; and even other libraries.

Solicitations for gifts need not be limited to the library's tax community or even to its region or state.
Tourist bureaus; travel agencies; foreign embassies; national or international organizations, foundations, or groups;
and even state or federal congressmen often can obtain free
materials for a library. A form letter or card requesting
free or inexpensive materials should be devised similar to
that shown in Figure 6.

Many gifts will be unsolicited and unwanted, though the librarian must be tactful in such a situation. Books cleaned from attics or garages and offered to the library may or may not merit inclusion in the library's collection. In order to maintain good will in the community yet still be able politely to refuse worthless books, the library should have a good written policy for the acceptance of gifts. A few general criteria for adding gifts to the collection or collections should be:

1. Gifts to the library should be judged on the same basis as purchased materials;

2. Gifts should have no special "strings" attached, such as a stipulation that the donated materials cannot be disposed of as other library materials or that the material must be kept in a special collection or location;

3. Gifts which are heavily worn, in need of extensive repair, or in poor or outdated editions when newer or better editions are available should not be added to the collection or collections.

Gifts also can be in the form of money to purchase new books or other items such as phonorecords, films or microfilms. Materials purchased with such money should be selected, ordered, received, and processed using the same criteria and procedures as for materials purchased from regular allocated funds.

Acknowledging gifts can be time-consuming if the job is not handled efficiently. A well-designed and neatly-reproduced form letter (see Figure 7) sent to a donor is not improper. For a gift of several books or other material, the individual titles need not be listed unless the donor requests an itemized list and their appraised value for deduction from his income tax.

```
                                  Anytown  Public  Library
                                  123  Bay  Street
                                  Zero,  Texas  78711

        Dear

        We would like to thank you for the gift of


        which you recently gave to the library.  These ma-
        terials will be classified and cataloged and placed in
        our permanent collection for the use and enjoyment
        of all.

        Sincerely,



        John B. Corbin
          Librarian
```

Figure 7. --A form letter which can be used to
acknowledge gifts to the library

If a very large or valuable collection is given, a
personal telephone call or a visit from the librarian would
be in order, perhaps with a personalized letter of thanks
following later. Any publicity given special gifts will aid
the library in general and will also encourage the donor and
others to continue their generosity to the library's programs
and collections.

A special book plate can be prepared and pasted in
gift or memorial items added to the library collection or
collections if so desired; normally, plates are placed in

books only, due to the unusual size and nature of such materials as periodicals, films, etc. This book plate can be
typed at the same time that acknowledgment is made of a
gift, then included with the material to be pasted in as
other processing steps are performed. Figure 8 is a sample book plate which can be placed in gift or memorial
books or other materials.

As gifts are received and approved for addition to
the library's collection or collections, the material can be
merged into the routines for processing purchased materials.
If multiple-copy order forms are used, a set can be typed
for each gift item and a part of each set inserted into the
"in process" file as a record. If multiple-copy order forms
are not used, an order card can be prepared for gift items.
In this case, care should be taken that "gift" is displayed
prominently on the card to avoid the possibility of the item
being included on a purchase order by mistake.

Exchanges. --Every library, whether large or small,
at one time or another will have unnecessary duplicate copies
of some material as well as other unwanted material. Many
libraries exchange duplicate copies and discards with other
libraries for material which is needed, often with no thought
of receiving anything in return immediately. A "one item
for one item" exchange arrangement also is common.

The main source of exchange materials will be other
libraries. Many local and regional "duplicate exchange centers" have been established throughout the nation, to which
libraries may send unwanted materials and exchange them
for wanted items.

The Duplicates Exchange Union, sponsored by the
Serials Section of the Resources and Technical Services

Figure 8.--A sample book plate which can be
placed in gift or memorial items

Division of the American Library Association, provides an
inexpensive, cooperative arrangement for the library to
share duplicate materials, as does the U. S. Book Exchange.

Exchanges also can be negotiated by personal contact,
telephone, correspondence, advertising in newspapers or library journals, or by special mimeographed or typed lists.
In many cases, a library can obtain material by paying only
the transportation costs from the library offering the material.

The criteria for adding exchanges to the library's
collection or collections should be the same as for gifts.
Acknowledgment of exchanges usually is not necessary.

As exchanges are received and approved for addition
to the library's collection or collections, the material can
be merged into the routines for processing purchased materials. If multiple-copy order forms are used, a set can
be typed for each item and a part of the set inserted into
the "in process" file as a record, or an order card can
be prepared as for gifts.

Choice of Vendors

Domestic In-Print Books. --It is usually best to
choose a jobber to handle the bulk of a library's book purchases. A jobber will sell the publications of many publishers, thus eliminating separate purchase orders by the
library to the various publishers and reducing the number of
shipments received and invoices to handle, check, and prepare for payment. A better overall discount, also, can
often be obtained through a jobber.

A jobber's discounts will depend to an extent upon
the amount of money a library plans to spend with him during a year and on the anticipated percentage of trade versus

technical and scientific titles to be purchased by the library.

Some books, such as publishers' reinforced editions (variously called "library bindings," "publishers' library bindings," etc.) and many technical and scientific titles are sold to a library with no discount; these are referred to as "net" or "net priced" books. Others, such as prebound books, usually are sold with a discount plus a pervolume charge for the special binding.

While the discounts allowed a library are one of the most important factors in choosing a jobber, other equally-important reasons are:

1. The length of delivery times for material ordered;

2. Whether the jobber will pay transportation charges on shipments (if the library must pay shipping costs, these could cancel virtually any discounts received);

3. The quality of billing by the jobber;

4. The quickness and willingness of the jobber to correct mistakes in shipping and billing;

5. The courtesy shown the library by the jobber;

6. The general integrity of the jobber and his representatives.

The librarian must remember that, just as he expects integrity, courtesy, and quality from a jobber, the jobber has the right to expect and receive the same from the librarian.

If dissatisfaction with the services of a jobber arises, the librarian should contact a representative of the firm and explain the situation. The jobber can perhaps rectify a disservice or misunderstanding. On the other hand, the librarian should not be fooled by empty promises; if a jobber constantly fails to live up to his stated terms, the librarian cannot afford to keep transacting business with him.

Not all titles can be ordered through a jobber. When a publisher refuses to sell to a jobber, the librarian has no choice but to order "direct" from the publisher. Other titles can be obtained faster and with better discounts when ordered in this manner. Experience will teach the librarian which titles should be obtained through his jobber and which from the publisher.

If there is a formal or written contract between the library and a jobber, such items as discounts to be received, the types of material which will be included in or excluded from the contract, and provisions for delivery times, cancellations, and reports on unshipped items should be included in the agreement.

Domestic Out-of-Print Books. -- Four common methods of obtaining out-of-print books are by:

1. Personally going to book stores which stock out-of-print items and searching for wanted items;

2. Searching through out-of-print dealers' catalogs for wanted items;

3. Advertising for wanted items in periodicals such as the Antiquarian Bookman;

4. Submitting a list of wanted items to a search specialist.

The latter method generally is least time-consuming and usually less expensive, though prices charged by different specialists for the same out-of-print item can vary widely.

A list of specialists in out-of-print materials can be found in the American Book Trade Directory, but there is no easy or safe method of determining which specialist

to use except by experience or contact with other librarians
who have used the services of a particular dealer.

Pamphlets. --Because they are similar in many ways
to books, pamphlets often can be included on an order for
books, if the jobber will agree to acquire them (or as many
as he can). Inexpensive (usually under $1. 00) and free
pamphlets which a book jobber can not or will not supply
must be ordered direct from the publisher or distributor.
Usually no or little discount can be expected on pamphlets.

Periodicals. --The process of acquiring periodicals is
somewhat different from that of acquiring books and pamphlets. When a book or pamphlet is ordered, received, and
paid for, the transaction normally is complete. A periodical subscription, on the other hand, is ordered or "placed"
and paid for, but the individual issues of the periodical will
arrive in the library over an extended period of time.

It is usually best to choose one vendor or jobber
(commonly referred to as a subscription or periodical agent)
to handle the bulk of the library's subscriptions. Such an
agent will handle subscriptions to most periodicals, thus
eliminating separate orders by the library to the various
publishers and reducing the number of invoices to handle,
check, and prepare for payment. A subscription agent can
sometimes obtain discounts on a list of subscriptions which
are unobtainable when orders are sent direct to the various
publishers, though such discounts will be quite small as
compared to those for books.

The choice of a subscription agent for periodicals
should be based on his ability to obtain subscriptions to the
bulk of a library's needs, his quickness and willingness to
arrange for missing or unshipped issues to be sent to the

library, the general quality of his service and his integrity, and any discounts which can be obtained on a subscription list.

The inexperienced librarian should study the stated terms in an agent's brochures, talk to a representative of the firm and, if possible, talk to other librarians using the same agent. Since subscriptions to periodicals are usually in effect for at least a year, the librarian cannot easily change agents during the year if dissatisfaction or disservice occurs; but subscriptions may be cancelled with that agent the second year if such a situation arises.

A list of periodical titles to which the library wishes to subscribe can be submitted to several agents for bids. When evaluating the submitted bids, the librarian should keep in mind that service is as important as any discounts offered.

Subscriptions to some periodicals cannot be handled by an agent. In such cases the librarian must order sub- scriptions "direct" from the publishers of the individual periodicals.

Newspapers. --While newspapers are similar to peri- odicals, in that a subscription is ordered or "placed" and paid for and the individual issues arrive in the library over an extended period, the methods of acquiring, receiv- ing, and handling them are somewhat different.

Some periodical subscription agents will handle news- paper subscriptions, but this service will rarely extend be- yond newspapers of national recognition or importance and usually only those which are issued on a weekly or bi- weekly basis and are similar in nature to a periodical.

As most small libraries will subscribe to few newspapers, it will be best to send separate subscription orders
"direct" to the individual publishers. For local newspapers,
telephone calls to the publishers can initiate the subscriptions.

Nonbook Materials. --Most book jobbers will not handle
nonbook materials. Special vendors will have to be located
or the materials ordered "direct" from the publishers, manu-
facturers, or their distributors.

Foreign Materials. --Ordering materials published outside the United States varies in difficulty depending upon the
country in which the material is published.

Canadian materials can be purchased through most
United States jobbers or can be ordered "direct" from the
particular publishers. American currency is acceptable in
most cases.

British publications are frequently published or distributed simultaneously in America and are obtainable easily
from most American jobbers or distributors.

There are many American importers who will obtain
or who maintain stocks of foreign and/or non-English language publications. A list of such importers and their
specialties can be found in the American Book Trade Directory.

Of course, a library can send orders "direct" to
publishers or other vendors in foreign countries. But dif-
ficulties arise with current addresses, price and currency
problems, language barriers, and delays in shipments.
Many foreign vendors discover that selling their publications
abroad is too difficult and will make little or no effort to do
so.

Standing and Blanket Orders. --A representative of
the library's regular book jobber should be asked if he will
handle standing and/or blanket orders. A jobber can handle
these orders for the publications of many publishers, thus
eliminating separate orders by the library to the publishers
and thereby reducing the number of shipments received and
invoices to handle, check, and prepare for payment. The
library placing standing or blanket orders with its regular
jobber usually can expect discounts on these orders to be
similar to the discounts received on publications ordered
through the normal acquisitions procedures.

If a jobber will not or cannot accept or handle standing or blanket orders, most publishers will accept such
orders "direct" from the library.

Preparation and Submission of Orders

After materials have been selected, requests for
purchase have been submitted to the technical services department, and the requests have been verified and searched,
then the requests are ready to be ordered.

Domestic In-Print Books. --There are several methods
of preparing orders to a vendor for domestic in-print books;
two common methods are:

1. To type each title to be ordered on a 3-by-5
    inch multiple-copy order form and to submit
    one or more parts of this form to the vendor
    as an order;

2. To type all titles to be ordered in a list form
    and to submit one or more copies of the list
    to the vendor as an order.

If the first method is used, a variety of "snap out"
multiple-copy order forms are available as stock items from
several library supply houses, or they can be custom-made
to suit the library's particular needs. These forms can be

a set of modified 3-by-5-inch order cards stubbed together
at the side or at the top, with carbon paper between the
parts or with the paper chemically treated to eliminate the
carbon paper ("ncr" or "no carbon required" paper).   The
number of parts in each set will vary, with five being the
most common.

The parts of a set should be of different colors, so
that those used for separate functions will be easily distinguishable from all others.   The last part of a set should
be of heavy paper or card stock, both to give the set "body"
as it is placed in a typewriter and to prolong this copy's
life if it is to remain long in an often-used file.

Standard multiple-copy order forms can be purchased
in single sets, in groups of two or three with perforations
between them for easy tearing apart, or in continuous "fan-
fold" lengths.   Since inserting them in a typewriter is time-
consuming, the more sets there are in a length of forms,
the more speed can be gained in preparing orders.

When in continuous lengths, the forms can be purchased with pin-feed or sprocket holes along each side, to
allow them to be used in a typewriter with a special platen
which will pull them through the machine easily, will keep
the forms aligned properly, and will eliminate the need to
constantly feed new sets into the machine.

The library's complete name and mailing address
should be imprinted on the set (if not on each part, defini-
tely on all copies that will be sent outside the library; for
example, on all parts that will be sent to the vendor as an
order).   Some library supply houses will imprint the forms
free, while others will charge for the special service.

Figure 9 illustrates several types of multiple-copy
order forms available as stock items from library supply

houses or on a custom-made basis. If Library of Congress
printed cards are to be ordered, the requirements of that
agency will dictate the design of the form to some extent
(see pages 149ff for a description of Library of Congress
cards and the procedures for ordering them).

One advantage of using multiple-copy order forms in
ordering is that one typing will produce several copies which
can be used simultaneously in separate files and in various
and different steps of ordering, cataloging and classification,
and further processing. One disadvantage is that the parts
are sometimes hard to handle and file and are lost easily.

The verified information on the order card submitted
as a request for purchase should be transferred to the
spaces reserved for the specific items on multiple-copy
order forms. Figure 10 illustrates the verified and searched order card shown in Figure 5 with all necessary information transferred to a multiple-copy order form, which then
is ready to be torn apart for further processing.

The parts of a multiple-copy order form are more
or less interchangeable, as long as each part is used consistently for the same purpose. If no use is found for any
one part of a set, that part can be discarded. If custom-
made forms are to be designed and printed, the exact number of parts required should be determined carefully before
the sets are prepared.

While it is impractical to enumerate the various
uses possible for the parts of a multiple-copy order form
set in technical services work, some common functions can
be described:

> 1. Vendor Order Copy or Copies: one or two
>   parts can be sent to the vendor as an order
>   (see below);

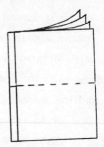

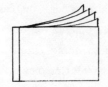

Side-Stubbed "one-up"
Multiple-Copy Order Form

Side-Stubbed "two-up"
Multiple-Copy Order Form
(Can be more than two)

Top-Stubbed "one-up"
Multiple-Copy Order Form

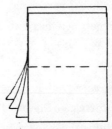

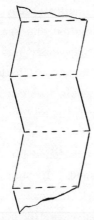

Top-Stubbed "two-up"
Multiple-Copy Order Form
(Can be more than two)

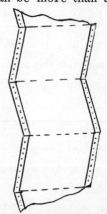

Continuous-Length Multiple-
Copy Order Forms

Figure 9.--Several types of
multiple-copy order forms
available as stock-items from
library supply houses or on a
custom-made basis.

Continuous-Length Multi-
ple-Copy Order Forms
with Pin-Feed Holes for
Use in Typewriter with
Special Pin-Feed Platen

	Ricard, Matthieu		OVER
	AUTHOR'S LAST NAME FIRST NAMES		
DO NOT WRITE IN THIS COLUMN	TITLE **Mystery of animal migration**		
DATE ORDERED **9-18-19XX**			
OF **Abel**	**Hill and Wang**		**1969**
	PLACE OF PUBLICATION PUBLISHER		YEAR
DATE OF BILL		CAT. NO.	**Booklist, Dec.1, 19XX**
COST	SECOND-HAND DEALER	ITEM	SOURCE OF DATA
POSTAGE:		**1**	**$5.95**
	EDITION VOLS.	COPIES	LIST PRICE EST. PRICE
ACCESSIONED	**General**		**Davis**
GG-1	FUND OR DEPT.	RECOMMENDED	COUNTERSIGNED

CLASS NO. **591.52**		L.C. CARD NO. **71-88011**	
LIST PRICE **$5.95**	AUTHOR **Ricard, Matthieu**		
DATE ORDERED **9-18-19XX**	TITLE **Mystery of animal migration**		
ORDER NO. **14-1647**	PLACE	PUBLISHER **Hill and Wang**	YEAR **1969**
DEALER **Abel**	VOLS.	SERIES	EDITION
NO. OF COPIES **1**			
DATE REC'D.	RECOMMENDED BY **Davis**	FUND CHARGED **General**	COST

Figure 10. --An order card shown with all necessary information transferred to a multiple-copy order form

2. Library of Congress Printed Card Order Copy:
   if Library of Congress printed cards are to
   be ordered, one part must be sent to that
   agency. A full description of this special
   part and its use is described in detail on
   pages 151ff. When returned with the printed cards, this part of the set can be used as
   a temporary shelf list card after cataloging
   and classification has been completed and before the permanent shelf list card is prepared;

3. Processing File Copy: one part can be filed
   into the "on order" file, then into the "in
   process" file when the book is received (see
   pages 153ff);

4. Vendor "On Order" File Copy: one part can
   be filed by order date or by purchase order
   number to await the receipt of the book (see
   pages 153ff);

5. "Rider" Slip Copy: one part can be forwarded
   as a "rider" slip as each title proceeds after
   receipt through the steps of processing. This
   part of the set can be the copy returned in
   the book when shipped by the vendor (see below);

6. Public Catalog Copy: one part (usually the
   last part, which is of heavier paper or card
   stock) can be filed in the public catalog as a
   notice that the book is on order. When the
   permanent catalog cards are filed after the
   book has been received and processed for
   the shelves, this part must be removed and
   destroyed.

Usually only one part of a multiple-copy order form
set is sent to a vendor as an order. If prior arrangements
are made to send two parts of a set, the vendor will insert
one copy inside the book when it is shipped to the library,
or will use one copy as a means of reporting to the library
if a book is out-of-print, out-of-stock, and so on. The
other copy will be for the vendor's use and probably will
never be returned to the library.

Multiple-copy order forms submitted as an order
should be arranged as recommended by the vendor (alphabetically by author, by title, or by publisher). If two parts
of a set are sent, both should be kept together but not
stapled or clipped together unless the vendor specifies differently.

Clear billing, shipping, and binding instructions
should be pre-printed on each form sent to the vendor,
typed or printed on a card placed in front of each group
of forms sent to the vendor, or negotiated and recorded
with the vendor in advance of any order being sent to him.

Billing instructions include requests that each invoice be submitted to the library in duplicate, triplicate,
etc. ; that discounts be taken individually from each title
listed on an invoice or from the final grand total amount
of the invoice; that any special binding or shipping charges
be included in the cost of each individual title, separately
at the bottom of an invoice, or on a separate invoice; and
so on.

Shipping instructions include the exact address where
shipments of books are to be delivered and an indication if
invoices are to be sent to the same or to a different address.

Unless otherwise instructed, a vendor will ship a book
in a cloth binding if available. If the library wishes that a
book be prebound, in a special library binding, or in a paper
edition, such instructions should be indicated on the order
form. It usually aids the vendor if orders for books to be
shipped in special bindings are separated and kept apart
from all other orders.

A group of order forms ready to be sent to a vendor
should be placed in a box for mailing or should be wrapped

securely in heavy paper and carefully sealed to prevent
damage to the forms.   Instructions for and restrictions on
mailing can be obtained from any post office.

If multiple-copy order forms are not used in ordering, then the books to be ordered can be listed on typing
paper or on a special form printed for this purpose.

The chief advantage of submitting lists of books to
be ordered rather than individual multiple-copy order forms
is that the lists are not as easily lost as are the smaller
individual forms, and all titles are displayed readily on
each order.   One disadvantage is that a list can be filed
only in one place, whereas parts of multiple-copy order
forms can be dispersed in several files.

If the list method of ordering is used, the verified
and searched order cards for the titles to be ordered
should first be arranged as recommended by the vendor
(alphabetically by author, by title, or by publisher); then
the necessary information is typed in a list form.

The information to be included for each title being
ordered will be similar to that on the order card with the
exception of the name of the person requesting the material
and the fund to which titles are to be charged.   In addition,
the extended price (the total number of copies of each title
being ordered multiplied by the list price per copy) should
be included beside each title.

A grand total of the extended prices should be typed
at the bottom of the last page of the order.   Figure 11 is
a sample list of books to be ordered from a vendor.   Figure 12 is a similar list of books to be ordered but typed on
a special order form printed for this purpose.

As when parts of multiple-copy order forms are submitted as orders, clear billing, shipping, and binding instructions should be included on each list order sent to a vendor or should be negotiated and recorded with him in advance of any order being submitted.

The number of copies to prepare of a list of books to be ordered will depend upon local policies and conditions. The original copy, with billing, shipping, and binding instructions attached or included, should be mailed to the vendor, and a copy should be retained in the technical services department. Additional copies may be filed in a separate business office within or outside the library as required by local policy.

Orders for domestic in-print books should be "placed" (or submitted) more often than once or twice a year to insure an even flow of new materials into the library. Staff time, the amount of the book budget, and the period in which the budget must be spent will dictate how often to order. Emergency orders can be placed at any time, of course.

Domestic Out-Of-Print Books. --A list of out-of-print books wanted by the library can be sent to an out-of-print dealer or a search specialist, or one or more parts of a multiple-copy order form can be sent in the same manner as for domestic in-print books.

The following information should be included for each out-of-print title wanted:

1. The author's surname and given names or initials;

2. The title of the book;

3. The edition number, if other than the first;

4. The publisher's name;

September 18, 19XX
Order No. XX-1687

Anytown Public Library
123 Bay Street
Zero, Texas 78711

Richard Abel and Company
3535 Dalworth Street
Arlington, Texas 76010

Gentlemen:

Please ship the following books to the above address.   Make
all invoices in duplicate, prepay all shipping charges and
add to your invoice.   Show our order number above on all
shipments and invoices.

Description	Copies	Price Each	Total
1. Bailey, W. R. Diagnostic microbiology. 2nd ed. Saunders, 1966.	1	$8. 25	$8. 25
2. Dudley, U. Elementary number theory. Freeman, W. H. , 1969.	2	8. 50	17. 00
3. Ibarra, F. Look and learn Spanish. Dell, n. d.	1	0. 60	0. 60
4. Ibarra, F. Spanish self-taught. Random House, 1941.	1	4. 95	4. 95
5. Keyes, K. Looking forward. Barnes, A. S. , 1969.	1	6. 00	6. 00
6. Roy, G. Road past Altamont. Harcourt, 1966.	2	3. 95	7. 90
7. Tilton, E. M. Union list of publications in opaque microforms. 2nd ed. Scarecrow Press, 1964	1	15. 00	15. 00
8. Tracy, M. Casserole cookery complete. Viking Press, 1956	1	2. 95	2. 95
			$62. 65

Sincerely,

John B. Corbin
Librarian

Figure 11. --A sample order for
books prepared in list form

TARRANT COUNTY JUNIOR COLLEGE DISTRICT   ORIGINAL

LIBRARY REQUISITION

TO   Richard Abel and Company
     3535 Dalworth Street
     Arlington, Texas 76010

DATE September 18, 19XX

SHIP ALL MATERIALS & INVOICE TO

LEARNING RESOURCES CENTER
TARRANT COUNTY JUNIOR COLLEGE
5301 CAMPUS DRIVE
FORT WORTH TEXAS 76119

ITEM	DESCRIPTION	COPIES	PRICE EACH	EXTENSION
1.	Brown, John R. Jacobean theatre. Putnam, 1967	1	1.65	1.65
2.	Chiara, Piero. Man of parts. Little, 1968	1	4.95	4.95
3.	Cowell, Joe. Thirty years passed among the players in England and America. Blom, 1968	1	12.50	12.50
4.	Gould, Joseph E. Challenge and change. Harcourt, 1969	2	1.20	2.40
5.	Hamilton, Thomas H. Democracy of excellence. Univ. of Hawaii, 1964	1	3.50	3.50
6.	Herburn, Andrew H. Rand Macnally guide to the midwest. Rand, 1968	1	1.95	1.95
7.	Jenyns, Soame. Background to Chinese painting. Schocken, 1966	1	2.45	2.45
8.	Keyes, Jean. History of women's hair styles, 1500-1965. Hillary House, 1968	1	3.50	3.50
9.	Lewis, Colby. Television director interpreter. Hastings House, 1968	2	8.95	17.90
10.	Oakes, George W. Turn left at the pub. McKay, 1968	1	4.95	4.95
11.	Simonson, Harold P. American perspectives. McGraw, 1968	1	6.50	6.50
12.	Wolfgang, Marvin. Studies in homicide. Harper, 1969	1	8.00	8.00
13.	Woodburn, John H. Teaching the pursuit of science. Macmillan, 1965	2	7.95	15.90

MAKE ALL INVOICES IN TRIPLICATE
PREPAY ALL SHIPPING CHARGES AND ADD TO YOUR INVOICE
TAX EXEMPTION CERTIFICATE NUMBERS AVAILABLE ON REQUEST
PLEASE SHOW PURCHASE ORDER DATE ON YOUR INVOICE

Total: $86.15

LIBRARIAN

Figure 12. --A sample order for books prepared
on a special form printed for this purpose.

5. The copyright date or date of publication;

6. The number of copies wanted.

Instructions to the dealer or search specialist should include:

1. Variations of the title wanted which will be accepted by the library; for example, if the same author and title is located but by a different publisher, in a different edition, or with a different publication date;

2. A limit on the price the library is willing to pay for any one item;

3. If the dealer or search specialist is requested to quote a price to the library before an item is shipped or billed;

4. A time limit for the search to continue;

5. Clear billing and shipping instructions to the dealer or search specialist.

Figure 13 is a sample list of wanted out-of-print books ready to be submitted to a dealer or search specialist. The original should be sent to the vendor and a copy should be retained in the technical services department.

It is best to send a list of wanted out-of-print books to one dealer at a time, but the list can be sent to several dealers at the same time. In this case, it should be clearly specified that price-quotes only are wanted until an official acceptance or an order from the library asking for shipment at an agreed-upon price is sent to a dealer. Otherwise, several copies of the same title may be shipped by several dealers at the same time.

Lower prices may be obtained for some items by asking for quotes from several dealers before books are shipped, but more correspondence on the part of the librarian will be required. Many dealers or search specialists will not accept a list unless it is given to them exclusively, at least for a

September 18, 19XX
Anytown Public Library
123 Bay Street
Zero, Texas 78711

Atkins Book Store
632 Fourth Avenue
New York, New York 10010

Gentlemen:

Our library would like to obtain the following list of out-of-print books. If you can locate any or all of these titles for under $10.00 each, please ship and bill to the above address in triplicate. If you can locate the same title by a different publisher, please ship the edition you can locate, if it is under $10.00. If you cannot locate any or all of these books by November 15, 19XX, we will consider the order cancelled.

1. Andrews, Joseph P. Book of the calendar. McGraw, 1955
2. Bishop, George F. Chants from the Aggies. Farm Press, 1943
3. Donaldson, Wilfred. Flowers in bloom. Foundation Pub., 1961
4. Peal, Daniel R. Introduction to logistics, 2nd ed. Wiley, 1945. Will accept any later edition found
5. Smith, Joseph M. Without a song. Editorial Press, 1967
6. Taylor, Mary P. Wallpaper samples. New Press. 1935.

We look forward to receiving as many of these titles as you can locate.

Sincerely,

John B. Corbin
Librarian

Figure 13. --A sample list of wanted out-of-print books ready to be submitted to a dealer or search specialist

certain length of time. They know that their efforts at searching, obtaining, quoting, and holding items might not be rewarded by a sale if they are only one of several dealers working on a list.

As out-of-print searches can take long periods of time and may never be fruitful, it is best not to send official purchase orders until books have been shipped and billed, or at least, not until they have been located, quoted, and accepted for shipment by the library.

If the librarian, while thumbing through a dealer's catalog of out-of-print items for sale, locates a wanted title, a letter or post card can be sent to the dealer asking for shipment of the title if it is still available. Figure 14 is a sample letter which can be used for this purpose (this form can be made into a post card just as easily, if desired). Again, proper billing and shipping instructions should be clearly stated.

When writing to an out-of-print dealer requesting shipment of a title or titles from a catalog, the librarian should indicate the catalog number (if any) and its date (if any), the item number of each book wanted, and the brief author and title of each book.

Since the library will be in competition with other individuals or institutions wanting to purchase the same item or items, speed in sending a request for shipment to a dealer is important. Out-of-print dealers routinely sell items listed in their catalogs to the first person requesting shipment. For this reason, if the technical services department is searching actively for many out-of-print items, all out-of-print dealers' catalogs should be searched thoroughly upon receipt and orders sent immediately, if wanted items are located at reasonable prices.

September 18, 19XX
Anytown Public Library
123 Bay Street
Zero, Texas 78711

Brumble's Book Store
955 North 75th Street
New York, New York 10035

Gentlemen:

I would like to request shipment of the following items from
your out-of-print catalog no. 15 dated September 1, 19XX,
at the prices stated in the catalog:

    Item 10: Jones, Lamont. History of taxes. $15. 00
    Item 44: Murphy, Gadston, Flower arranging for
                  beginners. $3. 00
    Item 80: Watson, James. How to make garden
                  furniture. $4. 00
    Item 82: Webster, J. H. English literature from
                  1800 to the present. $10. 00

If any or all of these are still available, please ship them
to the address above. Invoice in duplicate.

Sincerely,

John B. Corbin
Librarian

Figure 14. --A sample letter which can be used to
request shipment of out-of-print items from
dealers

Pamphlets. --The same procedures used by the technical services department to order domestic in-print books can be used to acquire pamphlets. If multiple-copy order forms are used to order books, then pamphlets can be ordered by the same method; if not, orders for pamphlets can be typed in list form or on the special form used to order books (see Figures 11 and 12).

When ordering pamphlets (particularly if they are free), many libraries by-pass the usual order procedures and send a post card or a form letter asking for a copy of the title. Figure 15 is such a form post card which can be used to request free or inexpensive pamphlets or other types of materials.

If pamphlets are free or relatively inexpensive and are not to be cataloged but placed in a pamphlet file (or "vertical file," as it is called in a library) in folders arranged by broad subject areas, most technical services departments will ask the selector himself to acquire, receive, and place the items in the files.

In the small library, enough flexibility should be maintained that some pamphlets can be acquired by the technical services department through its normal procedures and others can be obtained direct by the selector.

Periodicals. --Most libraries will "place" an order for the renewal of expiring periodical subscriptions plus any new subscriptions to be ordered only once a year, though more than one list a year is not uncommon.

Some libraries are required to renew their periodical subscriptions each year, while others are allowed to place them for two or more years at a time or on a " 'til forbid" basis, which means that a subscription once placed is

Anytown Public Library
123 Bay Street
Zero, Texas 78711

Gentlemen:

The Library would like to obtain the item(s) listed
below in the margin for which we understand there
is no charge.   If there is a charge and you will
accept stamps in return, please ship the item(s).
If there is a charge and you will not accept stamps,
please quote a price and we will send an order.

Sincerely,

Librarian

Figure 15. --A sample form post card used to request
free or inexpensive materials such as pamphlets

renewed automatically by the agent or publisher year after year
until the library or the agent or publisher terminates the arrangement.

The longer a list of subscriptions, the larger any
discount from the agent may be.   However, discounts on
periodical subscriptions have always been small, and the
discounts received on book orders should not be expected
at all.   Sometimes a savings can be obtained ,by the library
if subscriptions can be placed for two, three, or more years
at a time.

Ideally, all subscriptions to periodicals should begin
and end at the same time, to eliminate the preparation of
more than one list.   Subscriptions for the calendar year are
common, which means that the list should be submitted to
an agent sometime in October or November in order that he
can process the order and arrange for issues to begin arriving in the library in January.

Many school libraries require that their subscriptions
begin in September and end the following August, to coincide
with their academic year.   In this case, the list should be
submitted to an agent sometime in June or July in order
that he can process the order and arrange for issues to begin arriving in the library in September.

The minimum information for each title on a periodical subscription order should include:

1. The correct and latest title of each periodical;

2. The publisher or place of publication, if there
    are two periodicals with the same title or if
    there is reason to believe that there will be
    some doubt as to which title is wanted;

3. The period to be covered by the subscription;
    for example, "January-December 19XX;"
    "September 19XX-August 19XX;" etc. ;

4. The number of copies of each title wanted;

5. The cost of the subscription period per copy;

6. Whether each title is a renewal or a new subscription.

This information should be typed in list form or on a special purchase order form if used by the library (see Figure 12), arranged alphabetically by title. If desired, two lists can be prepared: one of renewals and one of new subscriptions. Figure 16 is a sample list of periodical subscriptions to be sent to an agent.

Clear billing and shipping instructions, requests for title pages and indexes, etc. , should be attached to or typed on the list.

The number of copies of a list of periodical subscriptions to prepare will depend upon local policies and conditions. The original copy, with billing and shipping instructions, should be mailed to the agent, and a copy should be retained in the technical services department. Additional copies may be filed in a separate business office within or outside the library as required by local policy.

Newspapers. --Most libraries will "place" an order for the renewal of expiring newspaper subscriptions plus any new subscriptions to be ordered only once a year, as for periodicals. Such a schedule is not as important as for periodicals, because fewer newspapers are subscribed to and virtually each renewal must be prepared as a separate order anyway. As with periodicals, a savings sometimes can be obtained by the library if a subscription can be placed for two, three, or more years at a time.

The minimum information for each title on a subscription order for newspapers should include:

September 18, 19XX
Anytown Public Library
123 Bay Street
Zero, Texas 78711

Dowder Subscription Agents, Inc.
57 Wilder Avenue
Washington, D. C.

Gentlemen:

Please enter the following periodical subscriptions for
us for the periods indicated:

1. Aerospace technology.   January-December
   19XX.   2 copies @ $6. 00 per subscrip-
   tion per year
2. Home appliance news.   January-December
   19XX.   1 copy @ $3. 00 per year
3. Journal of range management.   January-
   December 19XX.   1 copy @ $15. 00
   per year
4. Southern hardware.   January-December
   19XX.   1 copy @ $1. 00 per year
5. Trade trends.   January-December 19XX.
   1 copy @ $1. 00 per year
6. Yale University library gazette.   January-
   December 19XX.   1 copy @ $4. 00
   per year

All are new subscriptions.   Please ship all title pages
and indexes as they become available.   Submit your invoice to us in triplicate.   All issues should be mailed
to the "Periodicals Department" at the above address.

Sincerely,

John B. Corbin
Librarian

Figure 16. --A sample list of periodical
subscriptions to be sent to an agent

1. The correct and latest title of each newspaper;

2. The publisher's name and address;

3. The period to be covered by the subscription; for example, "January 1, 19XX-December 31, 19XX;" "September 1, 19XX-August 31, 19XX;" etc. ;

4. The number of copies of each title wanted;

5. For daily newspapers, an indication whether the subscription should include or exclude the Sunday edition;

6. The cost of the subscription period per copy;

7. Whether each title is a renewal or a new subscription.

This information should be typed in list form, on a form letter, or on a special purchase order if used by the library (see Figure 12). Figure 17 is a sample letter requesting the initiation of a newspaper subscription.

Clear billing and shipping instructions should be attached to or typed on the order.

As with books, pamphlets, and periodicals, local policies and conditions will dictate the number of copies of the order to be prepared. The original copy, with billing and shipping instructions, should be mailed to the vendor, and a copy should be retained in the technical services department.

Nonbook Materials. --When preparing orders for nonbook or "audio-visual" materials such as motion picture films, filmstrips, slides, phonodisc recordings, tapes, microfilm, microprint, microfiche, music scores, and so on, it is important that an accurate description of the desired items be given to the vendor. It is essential in some instances that vendors' catalog or stock item numbers be indicated.

Words and phrases such as "positive microfilm," "filmstrip, " "33 1/3 rpm phonodisc, " "18 x 24-inch oak-framed picture, " "miniature score, " and so on, should be

```
                                    September 18, 19XX
                                    Anytown Public Library
                                    123 Bay Street
                                    Zero, Texas 78711

Tampa Daily News
Rhatt Building
45 East Grand
Tampa, Missouri 64110

Gentlemen:

Our library would like to have a one-year subscrip-
tion to the Tampa Daily News, mailed to us, beginning
with the October 1, 19XX issue; please include the
Sunday edition in the subscription.  I understand that
the annual cost is $14. 50 by mail; if this is not cor-
rect, please bill us for the corrected amount.   This
is a new subscription.

Send your invoice in duplicate and mail the issues to
the "Periodicals Department" at the above address.

Sincerely,


John B. Corbin
Librarian
```

Figure 17. --A sample letter requesting the
initiation of a newspaper subscription

placed prominently beside each item on an order to avoid
shipping errors.   In most cases, purchase orders for different types of nonbook materials should be prepared separately.

Figure 18 is a sample order for microfilm. Orders
for other nonbook materials should be prepared in a similar
manner.

Clear billing and shipping instructions should be attached to or typed on each order.   The original copy, with
billing and shipping instructions, should be mailed to the
vendor, and a copy should be retained in the technical services department.

Foreign Materials. --The methods of preparing and
submitting orders for foreign materials are the same as
for domestic in-print books, the only difference being in
the vendor to which the order is sent.

Standing and Blanket Orders. --A form letter to a
jobber or publisher requesting that a title or titles be placed
on standing order will be sufficient.   If the list is long,
then it can be attached to a cover letter asking for the service.

The minimum information for each title on a request
for a standing order should include:

> 1. The author's surname and given names or ini-
>   tials (materials placed on a standing order
>   often will not have an author but an editor or
>   compiler which might change each year; in
>   this case, the author or editor might be omit-
>   ted entirely and the means of identification
>   will be the title);
>
> 2. The correct and latest title of the item;
>
> 3. The publisher of the title;
>
> 4. The number of copies of each volume, part,
>   year, etc. , wanted;

September 25, 19XX
Anytown Public Library
123 Bay Street
Zero,   Texas

Microfilms, Inc.
92 Washington Avenue
Washington, D. C. 20015

Gentlemen:

Would you please ship to us the following title on
positive 35MM microfilm:

    Tampa Daily News, 1900-1950.   30 rolls @
      $4. 00 per roll

Please ship the microfilm to the above address with
your invoice in quadruplicate.

Sincerely,

John B. Corbin
Librarian

Figure 18. --A sample order for microfilm

5. The volume, part, year, edition, etc., with
which the standing order is to begin.

The jobber or publisher should be requested to label
each shipment and invoice prominently as a standing order
to avoid confusing them with regular book orders. Such
special shipments then can be removed immediately from
the normal procedures for receiving books and can be ex-
pedited.

Clear billing and shipping instructions should be attached to or typed on each request for a standing order.
The original copy of the request should be mailed to the
jobber or publisher, and a copy should be retained in the
technical services department. Figure 19 is a sample request to a vendor asking for a standing order to be initiated
for a list of titles.

A blanket order with a jobber or publisher should be
negotiated carefully with a representative of the firm if possible. The subject area or areas to be included and excluded
in the arrangement should be defined clearly, and arrangements for the return of unwanted items and shipping and billing requirements of the library should be outlined and obtained in writing.

Receipt of Materials

Books. --When a shipment of books (domestic in-
print, out-of-print, or foreign) is received in the technical
services department, the shipping label or labels should
be checked to make certain that delivery was made correctly.
Damaged packages or cartons should be opened immediately
(if possible, before a bill of lading is signed) and inspected
for damage to the contents.

The books should be placed initially on a book truck
and should remain on this same truck throughout the

October 18, 19XX
Anytown Public Library
123 Bay Street
Zero, Texas 78711

Richard Abel and Company
35354 Dalworth Street
Arlington, Texas 76010

Gentlemen:

Would you please enter the following standing orders
for our library beginning with the dates indicated.
Invoice us in duplicate as you do for our other orders and ship to the "Acquisitions Department" at
the above address.   Please ship all standing orders
separately from our other orders and label each
box and invoice with "standing order. "

1.   New York Times Index.   New York Times.
     Begin with 19XX
2.   Oldmeyer, James.   Collected works.   Be-
     gin with volume 4
3.   Rand McNally World atlas.   Begin with
     17th edition
4.   Who's who in America.   Marquis Pub.
     Begin with 19XX-19XX

Please ship only one copy of each title.

Sincerely,

John B. Corbin
Librarian

Figure 19. --A sample request to a vendor asking
for a standing order for a list of books

processing steps to avoid unnecessary handling or moving
of the materials.

As the books are unpacked, care should be taken
that any packing list or invoice is not thrown away inadvert-
ently. While an invoice should be included in a shipment or
should arrive by separate mail at approximately the same
time, no further action should be taken until it is in hand.

The books first should be arranged in the order that
they are listed on the invoice.

If multiple-copy order forms are used in a vendor
"on order" file, the invoice for the shipment should be taken
to this file and all slips removed for the listed items.

The invoice should next be taken to the "on order"
file and all slips or cards removed for the listed items.
Each book received should be compared with its order records and the invoice to make certain that the correct title,
edition, volume, and number of copies have been shipped
and billed. The date of receipt should be stamped (an inexpensive band dater can be used) on the slip removed from
the "on order" file and this slip refiled into the "in process"
file or combined "on order-in process" file.

The slip removed from the vendor "on order" file
should have the date of receipt and the discount price (list
price minus any discount, plus any postage, handling, in-
surance, or binding charges) noted on it. This slip becomes
the "rider" slip, because it "rides" with each received book,
providing information already known about each and gathering
additional information as processing is completed.

If the books were ordered by typing them in list
order form, the copy of the order is removed from the
file, a check-mark is placed beside each item received,
and the order is refiled.

As each book received is compared with its order records and cleared, the item is checked off the invoice. If there are no errors in shipping or invoicing, the billing is checked for accuracy (preferably by adding machine) and the invoice is approved and forwarded for payment.

Invoices rendered in a foreign currency should be interpreted at the proper rate of exchange and the library's business office should be instructed as to the exact amount to be paid and where the check is to be sent. Any bank can give the current exchange rate for most countries' monies throughout the world.

After the order records have been pulled, checked, marked, cleared, and refiled, and the invoices have been cleared, approved, and forwarded for payment, then the books can be forwarded to the cataloging and classifying section for further processing. The "rider" slip with all information gathered to the moment should be inserted in each book where it can be seen easily.

Pamphlets. --The procedures for receiving pamphlets are the same as for receiving books. If pamphlets are included along with books or if they are included on a separate invoice, then the invoice can be cleared, approved, and forwarded for payment along with those for books. If a pamphlet is received free of charge, then there will be no invoice to prepare for payment, of course.

Small charges for pamphlets can sometimes be paid by stamps, petty cash, or money order, depending upon the policy of the library and the willingness of the vendor to accept this form of payment.

If a pamphlet is to be classified and cataloged and placed in the library's collection or collections along with

books, then the item can be forwarded if necessary to the
bindery section to be inserted into a pamphlet binder or
sent outside the library to be commercially bound before it
is processed further. The "rider" slip with all information
gathered to the moment should follow the pamphlet through
these steps and held in a file if the item is sent outside the
library for binding.

If a pamphlet is not to be classified and cataloged but
is to be placed in the vertical file, then the item can be forwarded immediately to the person in charge of the vertical
file. In this case, no slip should be placed in the "in process" file for the item.

Periodicals. --Individual issues of periodical subscriptions will be mailed to the library at more or less regular
intervals during the year. As each issue is received and
before it is unwrapped or processed further, the shipping
label should be checked to make certain that delivery was
made properly.

A subscription agent or a publisher will usually send
his invoice before issues of a periodical begin arriving in
the library, and the vendor will expect to receive payment
as soon as possible. Some libraries will approve the invoice for payment as soon as it is received, trusting that
the agent or publisher has entered the subscriptions as ordered and billed and will begin sending issues as designated.
Other libraries are not allowed to approve and pay an invoice
for periodical subscriptions until the first issue of each periodical has been received in the library.

In order to be certain that all issues of a subscription (even gift subscriptions) are received in the library,
some type of receiving record must be maintained. Usually

(but not always) the functions of receiving, recording, and
distributing the issues as they arrive are assigned to the
·technical services department.

As each issue of a periodical is received, a check-
mark should be placed on its check-in card in the appropriate box for the date of the issue (the check-in files for
periodicals are described on pages 92ff). If an issue has
a number (such as number 1, number 2, etc.) this number
should be used rather than a check-mark. Some libraries
prefer to record the issue number and the date of receipt
in the box. When the title page and index of a periodical
are received, these should be noted in the column designated
for this purpose ("t. p. and i" for "title page and index" can
denote this).

After issues of periodicals are received, unwrapped,
recorded in the check-in file, and rubber-stamped with the
library's ownership stamp, they should be forwarded immediately to the periodical display shelves or routed to
other destinations as noted in the check-in file.

It is imperative that the checking-in of periodicals
be accomplished rapidly as soon as they are received, in
order to have the issues on the display shelves to provide
the most current service to the library's users.

Newspapers. --Individual issues of newspaper subscriptions also will be delivered or mailed to the library at regular intervals during the year.

The payment of invoices for newspapers can be handled as for periodicals. For local papers which are delivered on a paper route, a request for special billing by invoice should be made to the publishers, unless the subscription can be paid from petty cash.

A modern trend in libraries is not to record the receipt of individual issues of newspapers, particularly if files of the back issues are not retained permanently or if the back-files are obtained on microfilm later. However, a check-in card can be prepared and maintained for newspaper subscriptions in the same manner as for periodicals.

After issues of newspapers are received, recorded in the check-in file (if one is maintained) and rubber-stamped with the library's ownership stamp, they should be forwarded immediately to the newspaper racks or to the person who maintains the files. It is imperative that the checking-in of newspapers be accomplished rapidly as soon as they are received.

Nonbook Materials. --The procedures for receiving nonbook materials are essentially the same as for books. Care should be taken to determine that material is not damaged in any manner before its invoice is approved and forwarded for payment.

After it has been determined that the correct items have been shipped, received, and billed, that the order records have been pulled, checked, marked, cleared, and refiled, and that the invoices have been cleared, approved, and forwarded for payment, the materials can be forwarded to the cataloging and classifying section for further processing.

Standing and Blanket Orders. --When a shipment of books on a standing or blanket order is received in the technical services department, the shipping label or labels should be checked to make certain that delivery was made correctly. Damaged packages or cartons should be opened immediately (if possible, before a bill of lading is signed) and inspected for damage to the contents.

If it can be determined readily that the shipment is
on a standing or blanket order (this should be noted on the
shipping label), the items should be removed from the main
job stream of receiving materials ordered through the normal
procedures.

The list of standing orders should be checked to make
certain that the titles received actually were requested on a
standing order basis.   If a check-in card is maintained for
the titles, then each volume, part, etc., and its date of
receipt and cost should be recorded in the same manner as
for periodicals.

Since orders for titles on a standing or blanket order
were initiated by form letters or lists rather than by official
purchase orders, there will be no multiple-copy order forms
or other slips to pull and process at this point.

A set of multiple-copy order forms (or an order
card, if multiple-copy order forms are not used) should be
prepared for each title received on standing or blanket order
in order that a record of each will be in the files.

The multiple-copy order form set is torn apart and
the parts placed in the proper files.   The part normally
forwarded to the vendor is destroyed and the part placed
in the vendor "on order" file is immediately placed in the
book as a "rider" slip.   No part is placed in the "on order"
file but one is inserted in the "in process" file, with the
date of receipt noted.

The total amounts on the invoices for standing and
blanket orders are checked for accuracy (preferably by adding machine) and the invoices prepared and forwarded for
payment.

Since a standing or blanket order was not initiated by
an official purchase order, one might have to be prepared
for the invoice; this will depend upon the accounting procedures and policies of the library or its business office. If
a confirmation order must be prepared, care should be taken
that, if a copy must be sent to the vendor, he understands
that it is to confirm a shipment already made; otherwise, a
duplicate shipment might be sent in error.

After its receipt and clearance, a title received on
standing or blanket order should be forwarded to the cataloging and classifying section for further processing like any
other book.

If an item received on standing order is part of a
set or series of which previous volumes, parts, years, etc.,
already have been classified and cataloged, the call number
on its check-in card should be indicated on the multiple-
copy order form before it is forwarded to the cataloging
and classifying section.

Return, Claiming, and Cancellation of Orders

Return of Orders. --If an error occurs in shipment
(wrong or defective item shipped, etc.), a letter asking for
correction should be written immediately to the vendor. A
form letter which can be used for a variety of problems
which will arise in ordering and receiving materials should
be designed, duplicated, and used to eliminate repetitive
typing of such letters. Figure 20 is a sample form letter
which can be used to ask for correction of several types of
errors.

Whenever an error is discovered on an invoice or in
a shipment and a letter has been written to the vendor asking
for a correction, then that invoice should be held in the

Anytown Public Library
123 Bay Street
Zero, Texas 78711

Gentlemen:

_____ The invoice for the item(s) listed in the margin below was (were) received over a month ago, but the material has not yet been received. Would you please forward the item(s) or inform us of the nature of the delay?

_____ The item(s) listed in the margin below was (were) ordered and received on our purchase order indicated, but no invoice has yet been received. Would you please forward the invoice or send a duplicate copy?

_____ The item(s) listed in the margin below was (were) ordered from you over 90 days ago on the purchase order indicated. We have neither received shipment nor a report. Would you please look into this matter and indicate when we may expect shipment or a report?

_____ Please cancel the unshipped item(s) listed in the margin below for the purpose indicated

_____ The item(s) listed below were shipped on our purchase order indicated but with the errors noted. We would appreciate a prompt correction of the error(s)

_____ The item(s) listed below on our purchase order indicated were listed on the invoice cited but the material was not received. Would you please ship them in order that we might process your invoice for payment?

_____ Other _____

_____

Sincerely,

John B. Corbin
Librarian

Citation(s):

Figure 20. --A sample form letter which can be used to handle a variety of problems in order work

technical services department until the proper shipment has been received or until a credit memo has been issued, unless previous arrangements have been made with the vendor for the handling of errors. For example, the vendor might allow the librarian to line through the billing for an item shipped in error or for a defective item, deduct the amount or amounts for the item or items from the invoice total, return the item or items in error with an explanation, then approve and forward the corrected invoice for payment. In this case, the vendor will reship and rebill the item or items in question at a later date.

If a title other than the one ordered is shipped and billed, it can be returned to the vendor with no preliminary inquiry, unless the library has agreed to substitutions. A note inserted in the material or an accompanying letter (the form letter in Figure 20 can be used) stating why it is being returned will aid the vendor in correcting the error and his records.

Defective material often will not be discovered until after the invoice has been paid and the material has been processed and is in use. A jobber, publisher, or other vendor will usually replace items found to be defective due to manufacturing errors, even though the library has already stamped and labelled them for use.

If, after receiving and paying for an item, someone discovers that the wrong title has been ordered or that it is otherwise unsuitable for the library's needs, a query to the vendor usually will result in permission to return the item for credit, providing that it is still in the same condition as when shipped. Most jobbers and publishers are anxious to please their customers.

Due to the distance and language barriers, returning foreign materials will be slower, but the procedures are the same as for domestic items.

Claiming Orders. --If an invoice for a shipment of materials is received in the technical services department but the items are not received within thirty days or so, or if an item is listed on an invoice but not received, then they must be "claimed" from the vendor. The form letter in Figure 20 can be used for this purpose.

If it is known that a volume, part, year, etc., of a title on standing order is available already but the library has not yet received its copy, then the form letter in Figure 20 again can be used to ask the vendor for shipment or for an investigation into the matter.

For many reasons, a library may often fail to receive particular issues of periodicals to which it has subscribed; these also must be "claimed" by the library. While the expected due-date recorded on the check-in card will be an aid in determining if an issue should be claimed or not, this is not an entirely reliable method. Production or mail delays can cause an issue to be late in arriving in the library. The most common method of locating issues of periodicals which should be claimed is to note if the previous issue was received when a new issue is being checked in. If the previous issue was not received, then it should be claimed.

An understanding should be reached between the library and its subscription agent whether missing issues should be claimed from him or from the publisher of the particular periodical. Once decided, the librarian should follow one method consistently. A form letter or card,

similar to that shown in Figure 21, should be used to claim
missing issues of periodicals.

The procedures for claiming newspaper issues are
the same as for periodicals. If an issue of a local paper
is not delivered, an immediate telephone call to the publisher
will be better than using a claim form similar to that in
Figure 21.

Cancelling Orders. --The technical services department should have an agreement (written or verbal) with its
vendors as to the time allowed for books, pamphlets, and
other materials to be shipped before they are reported on
or are automatically cancelled.

If a vendor has not supplied materials after a reasonable length of time (from sixty to ninety days) and has not
reported to the library that they are out-of-print, out-of-
stock, or will be shipped at a later date, then a query can
be made concerning the status of the orders. If the vendor
does not cancel the items, the librarian must decide whether
to leave them on order longer, to cancel and reorder from
another vendor, or to cancel and withdraw them from the
order processes.

Subscriptions to periodicals and newspapers are not
cancelled normally until the end of a subscription year, at
which time the particular titles simply should be omitted
from the renewal order to the agent or publisher, or a letter can be written asking for cancellation.

A standing order can be cancelled at any time by the
library, but the termination should be made as far in advance of publication as possible, to enable the publisher or
jobber to correct his files and stop shipment on subsequent
parts.

Anytown Public Library
123 Bay Street
Zero, Texas 78711

Gentlemen:

We note that we have not received the issues listed
in the margin below for which we have a paid subscription. Will you have this material forwarded
to us as soon as possible? If you cannot locate
our order, if the items are out-of-print, or if for
other reasons you cannot supply, please notify us.

Sincerely,

Periodicals Department

Figure 21. --A sample card which can be used to
"claim" missing issues of periodicals

Sets which are completed after a standing order is placed, of course, are considered cancelled automatically upon shipment of the last volume. For example, if a library places a standing order for a five-volume set and the five volumes have been published and shipped, then the arrangement is considered cancelled by the publisher or jobber. The librarian should remove the card from the "on order" file, from the standing order list, and from the standing order check-in file.

Maintenance of Files in Acquisitions Work

The "On Order" and "In Process" Files. --After an order is "placed" with a vendor, a record of each item should be inserted into an "on order" file. If multiple-copy order forms are used in ordering, one part of each set should be used as the entry record in this file. If multiple-copy order forms are not used, then the original order card prepared during the selection process should be used. The date that each item was placed on order should be noted on each of the slips in this file.

The arrangement of the slips in the "on order" file can be either alphabetically by author or by title. Most libraries arrange this file by author, but an arrangement by title is not uncommon.

The slips in the file should be maintained carefully in proper sequence, as misfiling can lead to "lost" records and to the possible duplication of orders. Enough guide cards should be placed in the file to reduce filing and finding errors.

After an item has been received, its record should be removed from the "on order" file, stamped with its date of receipt, and re-filed into the "in process" file. This

signifies that the material has been received in the library
and is being processed for the shelves.

The arrangement of the slips in the "on order" and
"in process" files should be the same, to provide uniformity
and to avoid confusion in their use.

After an item has been processed completely and is
ready for use, its "in process" slip should be removed from
the file and destroyed or placed in a "recent acquisitions"
file.   Care should be taken that the catalog cards have been
filed into the public card catalog before the slips are removed, in order that at least one record of the item is in
the library's files.

The "on order" and "in process" files can be combined into one, with the lack of a date of receipt indicating
an item's status as "on order" and the date of receipt indicating its status as "in process. "   In this case, the combined file can be referred to as the "order file. "

The Vendor "On Order" File. --If multiple-copy order
forms are used in ordering, a vendor "on order" file should
be maintained.   The part of the set which later becomes the
"rider" slip can be used as the entry record in this file.

This file contains a record of each item placed on
order with each vendor on each order date or with each
purchase order number.   It should be arranged either:

1. Chronologically by order date, then alphabetically by author or title;

2. Alphabetically by vendor, then chronologically
   by order date, then alphabetically by author or
   title;

3. Alphabetically by vendor, then numerically by
   purchase order number, then alphabetically by
   author or title;

4. Numerically by purchase order number, then
alphabetically by author or title.

Guide cards should be inserted between each order
for easy reference to the slips.

By consulting this file, the librarian can determine
the number of items placed on order with each vendor on
particular dates, the total number of items outstanding with
each vendor, or, conversely, the number of items placed
on order with each vendor which remain unshipped.

As items and their invoices are shipped by vendors,
the slips corresponding to the shipped items are removed
from this file.

Periodical Check-In File. --One of the best methods
of recording the receipt of the individual issues of periodical
subscriptions in the library is to utilize periodical check-in
cards.   One card should be prepared for each title received
(including gift or complimentary copies).   If more than one
copy of a title is received, a separate check-in card should
be prepared for each.   While the check-in cards can be arranged alphabetically by title in a card tray and removed
when needed and replaced afterwards, the most common
method of housing them is in a "visible file" or "visible index. "

According to Wulfekoetter:

> Perhaps the most widely known visible index is
> the Kardex file, made by Remington Rand.   It
> consists of a cabinet holding shallow metal trays
> which contain hinged cardboard leaves with slots
> in various positions, and provided with plastic
> pockets at the lower edge of each leaf.   Into the
> pockets and/or the slots in the leaves are inserted
> specially designed cards, the cardboard hinges on
> the leaves spacing them evenly so that the lower
> edge of each card is visible for easy location of
> desired titles. [2]

Figure 22 is an illustration of a visible file or index cabinet used to house check-in cards. The cabinets are available from a number of library supply houses in a variety of colors and sizes to meet every type of library's needs. A 3-by-5-inch check-in card is most common, but other sizes are available from many library supply houses or can be custom-made by most printers.

Some items of information which should be recorded for each periodical title are:

1. The correct and latest title of each periodical;

2. The publisher or place of publication, if there are two periodicals with the same title;

3. The frequency of publication (weekly, monthly, quarterly, etc.);

4. The name of the subscription agent or publisher (if ordered direct);

5. The expiration date of each title;

6. The current volume number of each title;

7. The location of each title in the library, if periodicals are not housed together in one central location in the building; for example, some periodicals might be placed in the reference room, some in a special browsing or lounge area, others in certain staff members' offices, etc.

Other items of information can be added to the check-in card (or to its back if necessary), depending upon the wish to make the visible file as useful as possible:

1. The cost of the subscription period per copy;

2. The date each issue of a title is expected to arrive in the library;

3. A list of the bound and unbound back-files of each title;

Figure 22. --A visible file or index cabinet
used to house periodical check-in cards

4. Routing notes, if certain titles are to be sent
   first to certain staff members or other persons before the issues are placed on the display shelves;

5. Binding information; for example, if issues of
   a title are to be bound when a volume is completed; when a volume is to be bound; if a
   title page and index will be received for a
   title; the color, type, and code number of the
   binding to be used.

Figure 23 is a sample check-in card for a monthly
periodical, and Figure 24 for a quarterly title. Cards for
other frequencies, such as semi-weekly, bi-monthly, etc.,
can be purchased or devised as needed.

Newspaper Check-In File. --If the receipt of the individual issues of a newspaper subscription is recorded,
then a check-in card similar to that for a periodical should
be used. The newspaper check-in cards can be housed in

TITLE — Practical Knowledge

CALL NUMBER

PUBLISHER OR AGN'T Nelson-Hall Pub. Co.

FREQUENCY M

ADDRESS 325 West Jackson Blvd.
Chicago, Illinois 60606
(direct)

BIND Yes

ROUTE Corbin

YEAR	VOL.	JAN	FEB	MAR	APR	MAY	JUNE	JULY	AUG	SEPT	OCT	NOV	DEC
67	5	No. 1	No. 2	No. 3	No. 4	No. 5	No. 6	No. 7	No. 8	No. 9	No. 10	No. 11	No. 12
68	6	No. 1	No. 2	No. 3	Not Pub.	no. 45	No. 6	No. 7	No. 9	no. 9	no. 10	no. 11	no. 12
69	7	No. 1	No. 2	No. 3	No. 4	No. 5	No. 6	No. 7	No. 8	No. 9	No. 10	No. 11	No. 12
70	8	No. 1	No. 2	No. 3	No. 4	No. 5	No. 6	No. 7	No. 8	No. 9	No. 10	No. 11	No. 12
71	9	No. 1	No. 2										

Practical Knowledge

TITLE

JAN | FEB | MAR | APR | MAY | JUNE | JULY | AUG | SEPT | OCT | NOV | DEC

Figure 23.--A sample check-in card for a monthly periodical

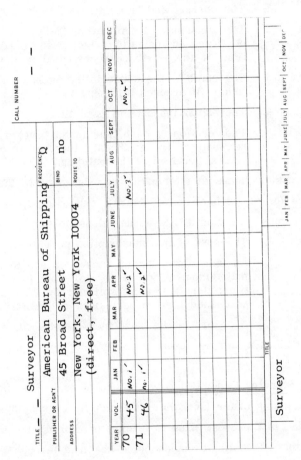

Figure 24.--A sample check-in card for a quarterly periodical

a special tray of the same visible file used for periodicals.

Some items of information which should be recorded for each newspaper subscription are:

1. The correct and latest title of each newspaper;

2. The frequency of publication (daily, weekly, etc.) and an indication whether the Sunday edition, if any, is to be received also;

3. The name of the subscription agent or the publisher (if ordered direct);

4. The expiration date of each title;

5. The location of each title in the library, if newspapers are not housed together in one central location in the building.

Other pieces of information can be added to the check-in card (or on its back if necessary), depending upon the wish to make the visible file as useful as possible:

1. The cost of the subscription period per copy;

2. An indication whether back-files are to be maintained or not; if so, for what length of time; if not, if a microfilm copy is to be purchased for the permanent collection;

3. A record of the back-files maintained, if any.

Figure 25 is a sample check-in card for a newspaper subscription.

Standing Order File. --A record of each title placed on a standing order (annuals, almanacs, etc.) should be recorded in the order files to eliminate or minimize the possibility of duplicate copies being acquired through the normal ordering procedures.

A card placed permanently (or, until the standing order is cancelled) in the "on order" file indicating that a title is on standing order will aid the librarian to avoid duplicating the order. A list of titles on standing order also can be placed near the order files for quick reference as new requests are being processed for purchase.

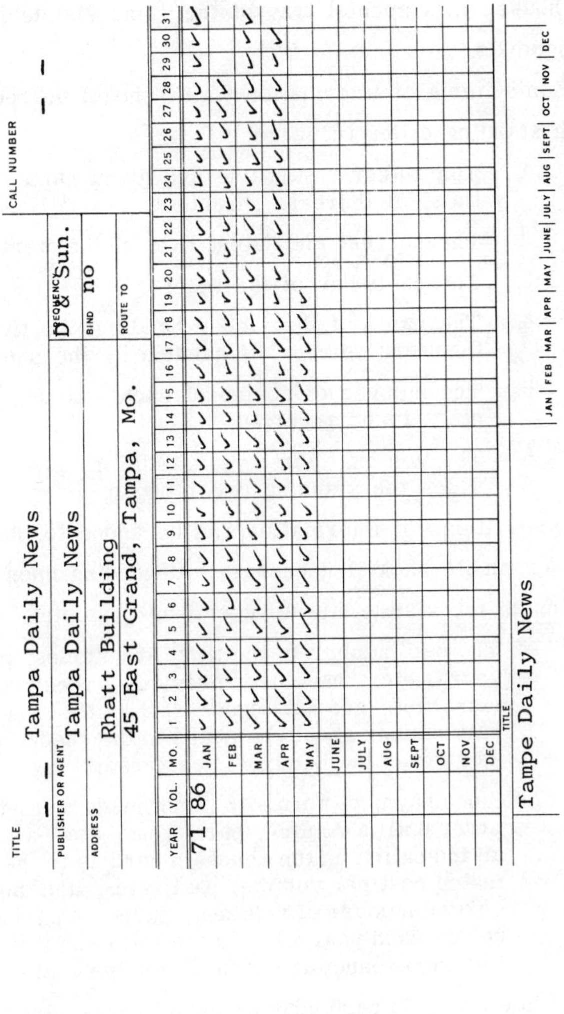

TITLE
Tampa Daily News

CALL NUMBER

PUBLISHER OR AGENT
Tampa Daily News

FREQUENCY
D & Sun.

ADDRESS
Rhatt Building
45 East Grand, Tampa, Mo.

BIND
no

ROUTE TO

YEAR | VOL. | MO. | 1–31
71 | 86 | JAN, FEB, MAR, APR, MAY, JUNE, JULY, AUG, SEPT, OCT, NOV, DEC

TITLE
Tampe Daily News

JAN | FEB | MAR | APR | MAY | JUNE | JULY | AUG | SEPT | OCT | NOV | DEC

Figure 25. --A sample check-in card for a newspaper subscription

A simple means of recording the receipt of each
volume, part, year, etc., of a standing order is to use a
check-in card similar to that for a periodical. These cards
can be housed in a special tray of the same visible file used
for periodicals.

Some items of information which should be recorded
for each standing order title are:

1. The author's surname and given name or ini-
    tials, if there is an author;

2. The correct and latest title of the item;

3. The publisher of the title;

4. The name of the jobber handling the title or
    the word "direct" if handled by the publisher;

5. The number of copies of each volume, part,
    etc., to be received;

6. The volume, part, year, edition, etc., with
    which the standing order began.

Other items of information can be added to the check-
in card (or on its back if necessary), depending upon the
wish to make the visible file as useful as possible:

1. The call number of the title, if volumes, parts,
    years, etc., have been previously received,
    classified, and cataloged. If the title is new, the
    call number should be added to the check-in card
    as soon as the number is assigned;

2. Since payment normally is not made on a standing
    order until a volume, part, year, etc., is received,
    an indication on the check-in card as to the esti-
    mated cost per volume, part, etc., and the anti-
    cipated number of volumes, parts, etc., to be re-
    ceived each year will aid the librarian in estima-
    ting the expenditure of funds for the year.

Figure 26 is a check-in card adapted for a title received on a
standing order basis.

Miscellaneous Files. --If orders to vendors are typed
in list form, a copy of each should be retained in the

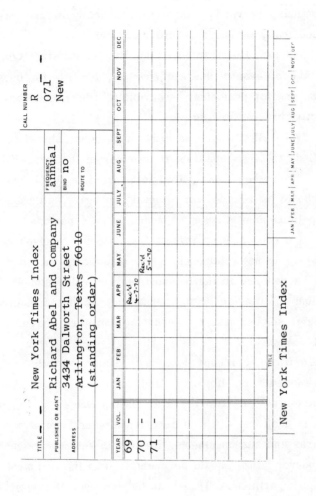

Figure 26. --A check-in card for a title received on standing order

technical services department, arranged either chronologically
by date of order; numerically by purchase order number; or
alphabetically by vendor, then chronologically by date of order
or numerically by purchase order number.

Separate files can be maintained for different types of
materials for ease of use; for example, one file for book
orders, one for periodical subscription orders, one for
microfilm orders, and so on.

When all titles on an order have been shipped or
cancelled, the list should be removed from the active file,
marked "complete," and placed in an inactive file. These
files should be retained for at least two years, although
local policies may dictate other maintenance periods.

If a copy of each invoice for material received in
the library is not retained in a file elsewhere, then a copy
should be retained in the technical services department.
Occasions often arise in this department when copies of invoices for shipped materials must be consulted and/or
copied.

A file of correspondence with dealers, publishers,
agents, individuals, librarians and instituions should also
be kept for at least two years or until inactive.

In addition, a file of recent publishers' catalogs,
brochures and announcements, for use in selection, searching, and verifying, should be maintained in the technical
services department. These can be arranged alphabetically
by publisher in pamphlet boxes or in unused slip-case boxes
in which books have been shipped. As new or revised
catalogs, brochures, and announcements are received, super-
seded copies should be pulled from the files and discarded.

Notes

1. Gertrude Wulfekoetter, Acquisition Work: Processes Involved in Building Library Collections (Seattle: University of Washington Press, 1961), p. 3.

2. Ibid., p. 216.

CLASSIFICATION AND CATALOGING OF MATERIALS

In order for a collection or collections of materials to be useful and usable to librarians and other users of a library, its materials must be classified or arranged according to subject or type of materials, cataloged or described in a standardized manner, and cross-indexed to allow users to locate specific items rapidly by author, by title, by subject, by classification number, and so on.

This indexing of materials in a library and the preparation and maintenance of the indexes (the card catalog and the shelf list) are among the most complex and difficult functions of the technical services department. They, like the administration of the department, require the attention of qualified and trained librarians, though much of the work can be accomplished by adequately trained and properly supervised nonprofessionals.

Classification of Materials

The classification of library materials is "the assigning of books and other materials to their proper places in a system of classification."[1] A system of classification is a "... scheme for the arrangement of books and other material according to subject or form."[2]

Two prime functions of a classification system are:

1. To serve as a device to group and maintain materials in a logical order on the shelves;

2. To serve as an aid to identify and locate these materials on the shelves.

Classification Systems Available. --There are several
systems of classification available to libraries for arranging
their collection or collections.   The two most commonly-used
in the United States are the Dewey Decimal Classification
(DDC) and the Library of Congress Classification (LC).

Melvil Dewey first devised his system in 1873, and
it has gone through many changes and editions since then (the
17th unabridged edition was published in two volumes in 1965 *18th*
and 1967 and contained 1, 254 and 1, 226 pages, respectively). *1972*
Dewey wanted a system "which would be simple and which
could be adapted in most libraries because of its ease of
application, expansibility, and general appeal. "[3]

He accomplished his purpose, for most school, public, and college libraries in the United States and many
abroad soon adopted his scheme and continue to use it to
this day.   But many small libraries discovered that the unabridged edition, as it grew in size and complexity to meet
the demands and needs of large libraries, was too detailed
and overwhelming for their small collections.   So an unabridged edition was prepared for them (the 9th abridged
edition was published in 1965 with 594 pages).

Dewey's Decimal Classification system divides all
knowledge into ten main subject groups:

000	General Works
100	Philosophy
200	Religion
300	Social Sciences
400	Philology
500	Pure Science
600	Useful Arts
700	Fine Arts
800	Literature
900	History

Each of these ten main groups or "classes" of

knowledge can be further divided into ten additional, more
narrow subject groups.   By incrementing the second digit
from the left of, for example, the "800" group, all literature can be divided in this manner:

800   Literature

810   American Literature
820   English Literature
830   German Literature
840   French Literature
850   Italian Literature
860   Spanish and Portuguese Literature
870   Latin Literature
880   Greek Literature
890   Other Literatures

In turn, each of these ten sub-groups or sub-classes
can be further divided into ten additional, more narrow
groups.   By incrementing the third digit from the left of,
for example, the "810" group, all American literature can
be divided in this manner:

810   American Literature

811   American Poetry
812   American Drama
813   American Fiction
814   American Essays
815   American Oratory
816   American Letters
817   American Satire and Humor
818   American Miscellany
819   Canadian English Literature

Any item classified according to the Dewey Decimal
Classification system must be assigned a minimum of three
numeric digits; for example, "008" (not "8"), "090" (not
"90"), "799, " and so on.

If further division of a classification number is necessary, a decimal point is introduced after the third digit of
the number and the division continues.   Thus a classification

number (using the unabridged edition) can be quite lengthy
and complex; for example, a book on the subject of veteri-
nary pharmacology could be properly assigned this number:
"636.0895328"; however, most libraries would cut the number to "636.089" or, in the very small library, "636."

It readily can be seen that the first (or left-most)
digit in a Dewey Decimal Classification system number ar-
ranges material in the broadest of subject groups, and that
each digit to the right of this first number further categor-
izes an item in a narrower and narrower subject division
until the proper "depth" of classification is reached.

The "depth" of classification must be defined by the
individual library and will depend upon:

1. The size of its collection or collections of
    materials and the subject emphasis of the li-
    brary; or, to be more exact, the number of
    anticipated titles in any one subject area;

2. The philosophy or desire of the library to
    group materials loosely in broad subject
    areas only or in narrow, specific areas.

The Library of Congress Classification system has
evolved from many decades of work at the Library of Congress in Washington, D.C., to organize its collections into
logical and usable arrangements. While the system is based
on, and has its roots in, many other classification schemes,
it is designed specifically for the Library of Congress and
for no other. However, other libraries--particularly those
with large collections--have found the system usable and
have adopted it.

This classification system divides all knowledge into
main subject groups as does the Dewey Decimal Classification system, except that letters of the alphabet are used as
the primary dividers:

A	General Works; Polygraphy
B	Philosophy; Religion
C-D	History (Except American); Genealogy
E-F	American History
G	Geography; Anthropology
H	Social Sciences
J	Political Science
K	Law
L	Education
M	Music
N	Fine Arts
P	Language and Literature
Q	Science
R	Medicine
S	Agriculture
T	Technology
U	Military Science
V	Naval Science
Z	Bibliography and Library Science

The system constantly is undergoing scrutiny and revision to provide a viable and flexible scheme; therefore, many gaps have been left vacant for further expansion. For example, the letters, "I," "O," "W," "X," and "Y," have not been utilized as main subject divisions yet.

Each of the main groups or "classes" listed above can be further divided into additional, narrower subject groups; for example, by adding a second alphabetic letter to the right of that for the main group or class, all science literature can be divided in this manner:

Q	Science (General)
QA	Mathematics
QB	Astronomy
QC	Physics
QD	Chemistry
QE	Geology
QH	Natural History
QK	Botany
QL	Zoology
QM	Human Anatomy
QP	Physiology
QR	Bacteriology

In turn, each of these sub-groups or sub-classes
can be further divided by adding a series of numeric digits
ranging in number from one to four, which further divides
each area of knowledge; for example, "QC" or "physics"
can be divided in this manner:

QC	Physics	
QC	81-119	Weights and Measures
QC	122-168	Experimental Mechanics
QC	811-849	Terrestrial Magnetics
QC	851-999	Meteorology

The missing numerals have been left for expansion as new
or different knowledge emerges or as other divisions need
expanding.

Occasionally, the numeric division will have a sub-
division of its own; for example:

DA	566.5
E	312.7
E	322.72
QD	151.5
	etc

Most of the groups or classes of the system can be
further divided by geographical location, by form or type
of material, by the individual titles of authors or by several
other methods. These last notations are indicated by a combination of special, alphabetic and numeric characters based
on specially-prepared tables of numbers and by Cutter letters and numbers (see below for a description of Cutter
numbers). Detailed schedules indicating the main groups
or classes, sub-classes, special tables, and subject indexes to the groups have been published and are available
from the Library of Congress or from the U.S. Government
Printing Office.

As an example, "Z1242. 5. F85" is the Library of
Congress Classification number for a bibliography of the
Confederate States of America written by Douglas Southall
Freeman. This could have been written and explained in
this manner:

Z	=	Bibliography and Library Science
1242	=	American Bibliography: History and Description: Civil War, 1861-1865
. 5	=	Confederate States of America (Imprints)
. F	=	Author Letter Representing the First Character of "Freeman"
85	=	Author Number (Cutter Number) Representing the Remainder of "Freeman"

As each new title is classified in the Library of
Congress, its number is checked carefully against all classification numbers previously assigned in the past to materials. By the addition or interpolation of numbers, no two
titles will ever have the same classification number.

Author Letters and Cutter Numbers. -- For those libraries using the Library of Congress Classification System, each classification number is unique in itself; therefore, copies of the same title simply can be labelled as
"copy 1, " "copy 2, " etc. , or each can be assigned a unique
accession number to distinguish the copies.

But if the Dewey Decimal Classification system is
used by the library, then all titles (and copies of the same
titles) on the same subject will be assigned the same classification number. For example, all books on algebra would
have the same Dewey Classification number, "512. " Thus,
the books would be shelved together as desired by subject,
but individual titles and copies within the subject could not
be maintained in any kind of order, particularly if the library has many books on the same subject.

As a library grows, the need to provide accountability of materials and to provide a unique "call number" for each copy of a title in the collection or collections increases. Also, as the collection or collection grows, keeping books in proper order on the shelves and locating them on the shelves becomes increasingly difficult.

In order to maintain items assigned the same Dewey Decimal Classification number in correct order on the shelves, some libraries place the first one, two, or three letters of the authors' surnames under the classification number and arrange titles with the same Dewey number by these "author letters;" for example:

574.2	;	574.2	;	574.2	;	574.2	;	etc.
A		A		M		W		
574.2	;	574.2	;	574.2	;	574.2	;	etc.
Ad		Am		Mi		Wa		
574.2	;	574.2	;	574.2	;	574.2	;	etc.
Ada		Ame		Min		Was		

In a small library, any of these methods used consistently will be adequate, since there will be relatively few books in any one classification number. Consequently, a particular book will not be difficult to locate on the shelves within a subject area.

The combination of the Dewey Decimal Classification number and the author letter or letters described above still will not provide a unique "call number" for each title. For example, as the number of items within a subject area increases further, there could be several or many titles with the call number 574.2 or 574.2 or 574.2 (whichever
                          A   Ad   Ada
is used).

why not cp?

In this case, the only certain method of distinguishing the items is to assign each copy of a title a unique
accession number and to use the number in conjunction
with the call number to identify each uniquely.

To alleviate this problem to some extent, some libraries use a "book number" in conjunction with each
classification number assigned to a title. A book number
is a "combination of letters and figures used to arrange
books in the same classification number in alphabetical
order."[4] This number is composed of three distinctive
parts:

1. An alphabetical letter or letters representing
   the first or first few letters of the surname
   of the author of a book or other material;

2. A series of numbers that represent the re-
   mainder of the author's surname;

3. A "work mark" used to distinguish different
   titles by the same author with the same
   classification number.

Three aids commonly used to prepare book numbers
are the Cutter two-figure tables, the Cutter three-figure
tables, and the Cutter-Sanborn three-figure tables; the use
of the Cutter three-figure tables is described below as an
example.

To determine the Cutter number for an author, the
first few letters of his surname are located in the tables,
and the corresponding numbers are added to the author
letter or letters. For example, if the Cutter number for
"Cerfman" is to be determined, the portion of the tables
in the vicinity of the name is:

333	Cent
334	Cer
335	Cerf
336	Cerr
337	Cers

The numbers, "335," are the closest to "Cerfman" (or "Cerf") and become the Cutter numbers for the author. These numbers are added to the author letter ("C" for "Cerfman") and become the author number, "C335."

For another example, if the Cutter number for "Cereman" is to be determined, one will discover that "Cere" is not in the tables. In this case, the numbers directly above the closest entry to "Cere" are used. These numbers are added to the author letter ("C" for "Cereman") and become the author number, "C333."

If, after checking in the shelf list, the cataloger discovers that a Cutter number already has been assigned to another author, a fourth number should be added for the new author, as described by Cutter:

> If the number found is already in use, annex another decimal. E. G., if there is a Harris, Ferdinand H241, Harris, George may be numbered with a fourth figure, H2414; Harris, Frank H2411; Harris, Henry H2416; Harris, Isaac H2418. This can be carried to any extent. [5]

The numeral "1" is avoided as long as other numbers are vacant, because, once used, nothing can be inserted before it, and the numeral "O" should be used only in extreme cases.

A work mark is a lower-case alphabetic letter added to an author number to distinguish one title by an author from another title by the same author when both titles have the same classification number. The first letter of a title, omitting any initial article, serves as the work mark.

For example, the call number of The History of Mathematics by David Jones could be $\frac{510}{J713h}$, while that for Mathematics Today by the same author could be $\frac{510}{J713m}$.

In the event that two titles by the same author with the same classification number have the same initial letter, then the second letter of the title must be added to the work mark for one of the titles (usually the last one added to the collection).

For example, the call number of The History of High School Algebra by David Jones could be $\frac{512}{J713h}$, while that of The History of College Algebra by the same author could be $\frac{512}{J713hi}$.

Special Classification Numbers and Symbols. --There are several special classification numbers or symbols commonly used in libraries (particularly in public and school libraries), notably those for fiction, juvenile, young adult, easy, short collections, biography, and reference books.

Instead of assigning the Dewey or Library of Congress classification numbers to books of fiction, some libraries will arrange these alphabetically by author and use "F" or "Fic" for fiction as the "classification number" or symbol.

In a public library, books written specifically for certain age groups should be assigned special symbols in addition to the regular classification numbers to distinguish them from adult books. The common symbols are "J" or "Juv" for "juvenile" and "Y" or "YA" for "young adult" books; for example;

      J   or Juv   Y   or YA
     364. 2   364. 2 ; 917. 2   917. 2

Books of fiction for juveniles or young adults can have these same symbols over "F" or "Fic" for fiction; for example:

(handwritten margin note: not really class. no. grouping devices)

J or Juv ; Y or YA
F   Fic   F   Fic

"Easy" books are characterized by their simplified
writing and pictures designed for children unable to read or
just beginning to read. For this reason, "easy" books are
usually not classified but are only assigned an "E" for
"easy. "

Collections of short stories written by two or more
authors can be arranged alphabetically by editor or compiler
and assigned the symbols "SC" for "short collections" or
"SS" for "short stories. " Short stories may be for adults,
juveniles, or young adults; for example:

SC or SS; J   or Juv or J or Juv; Y or YA
                SC   SC   SS   SS   SC   SC

or Y   or YA
   SS   SS

Three methods of classifying biographies or auto-
biographies of individuals are to use either "B" for "biography"; "921" (the correct Dewey Decimal Classification
number); or "92" (a shortened form of "921"). For biographies of two or more people, "920, " the Dewey number
for collective biography should be used.

Most libraries have collections of materials such as
encyclopedias, dictionaries, handbooks and almanacs, which
are shelved separately from materials which can be "charged
out" or taken from the library. These noncirculating titles
are assigned an "R" or "ref" for "reference" above the regular classification number to distinguish them from materials
which circulate; for example:

R   or Ref ; R   or Ref; R   or
810. 8   810. 8   031   031   E185. 1. R25

Ref
E185. 1. R25

When titles are assigned special classification numbers or symbols, author letters or Cutter numbers can be used in the same manner as described above to complete and form a unique "call number" for each; for example:

F or	Fic or	Fic or	F or	Fic
A	Ad	Ada	A27h	A27h

J or	Juv or	Juv or	J or	Juv
F	Fic	Fic	F	Fic
A	Ad	Ada	A27h	A27h

Y or	YA or	YA or	Y or	YA
F	Fic	Fic	F	Fic
A	Ad	Ada	A27h	A27h

J or	Juv or	Juv or	J or	Juv
574.2	574.2	574.2	574.2	574.2
C	Ae	Cer	C863h	C863h

Y or	YA or	YA or	Y or	YA
574.2	574.2	574.2	574.2	574.2
A	Ad	Ada	A27h	A27h

R or	Ref or	Ref or	R or	Ref
810.4	810.4	810.4	910.2	910.2
A	Ad	Ada	A27h	A27h

A biography of an individual is treated somewhat differently, in that the first one, two, or three letters of the person written about is used instead of the letter or letters of the surname of the author. If a work mark is assigned, the first letter of the surname of the author is used. Thus a biography of Roosevelt written by John Doe could have the following numbers:

92 or	92 or	92 or	92 or	B or	B
R	Ro	Roo	R677d	R	Ro

or B or	B or	921 or	921 or	921 or	921
Roo	R677d	R	Ro	Roo	R677d

Cataloging of Materials

The cataloging of library materials has been defined as "the process of preparing a catalog, or entries for a catalog."[6] An entry is a record of a book or other material in a catalog.

There are two types of cataloging, or, rather, two phases of cataloging which are distinguishable: descriptive cataloging and subject cataloging.

Descriptive Cataloging.--Descriptive cataloging is defined as "that phase of the process of cataloging which concerns itself with the identification and description of books."[7]

This infers, simply, that a book or other material is described in a standardized form and sequence by its author, editor, or compiler; title; edition; imprint; collation; and notes, in such a manner as to distinguish it from every other item in the library's collection or collections.

Descriptive cataloging can be either detailed or simplified. For the small-to-medium sized library, simplified cataloging is preferred--not only because it is debatable whether detailed cataloging is essential in a small library, but because detailed cataloging is complex, costly, and time-consuming if it must be prepared locally.

A brief description of simplified descriptive cataloging is given below (see also Figure 27). Susan Grey Akers' Simplified Library Cataloging, Margaret Mann's Introduction to Cataloging and the Classification of Books, Paul Dunkin's Cataloging, USA, and Esther J. Piercy's Commonsense Cataloging, and several others should be consulted for more complete information. Citations for these and other aids are given at the end of this manual.

The first item in descriptive cataloging is the author statement, which consists of the name of the author, editor, or compiler chiefly responsible for the issuance of a title. The name on the title page of an item will be that most likely to be used (see Figure 27).

Should two or more persons be the authors, editors, or compilers of a title, the name listed first on the title page is used in the author statement. If a corporate body is chiefly responsible for the issuance of a title, then that body's name is considered to be the author and is so recorded as the entry.

Birth and death dates of an author and such words as "sir," "dr.," "mrs.," and so on can be omitted in simplified cataloging for the small library.

In the case of a title whose editor or compiler changes frequently, such as a yearbook or almanac, the item is treated as if it had no author and is referred to as a "title entry."

The second item in descriptive cataloging is the title statement, which consists of the title of an item, with the same wording and spelling as appears on the title page. Unless the title itself is meaningless without it, a sub-title can be omitted from the description (see Figure 27).

In simplified cataloging, the statement of authorship is repeated after the title only if it is necessary. The cases in which the author should be repeated are described in Chapter 6 of Akers' Simplified Library Cataloging.

The edition of a title is included after the title or after the statement of authorship (if included after the title). If a title is in its first edition, no note of the edition is made (see Figure 27).

always

In detailed descriptive cataloging, the imprint consists of the place of publication, the complete name of the publisher, and the copyright date or date of publication (or both) of a title.

In simplified descriptive cataloging, the place of publication is omitted completely from the imprint. If two or more publishers are listed on the title page, only the first or the first American publisher is listed. Initials and words such as "publisher," "and sons," "inc.," and "and company" are omitted from a publisher's name (see Figure 27).

The latest copyright date, shown on the back of the title page, is used as the date of publication; for example, "c1970," "c1968," etc. If no copyright date is indicated and none can be determined from other sources, the date on the title page is used without a "c" before it. If no date at all can be found, the abbreviation, "n. d.," for "no date" can be used.

The collation includes the number of pages of a one-volume title or the number of volumes of a title in more than one volume and information about its illustrations (see Figure 27).

The number of pages of a title is indicated in Arabic numbers, followed by the abbreviation, "p," for "pages;" for example, "102p.," "563p.," etc. If the pages are unnumbered, the word, "unpaged," or "lv," for "one volume" can be used.

If a title has more than one volume, the total number of volumes is indicated instead of the number of pages, regardless of the paging in the separate volumes; for example: "2v.," "3v.," etc.

Jones, William Batford
    The influenced years; America prior
to the Civil War.   3rd ed.   Scribner,
c1970.
    532p.   illus.   (The history of America
series)

Figure 27. --An author card illustrating
simplified descriptive cataloging

The following explains the illustration statement:

The abbreviation 'illus.' for 'illustrations' is used to describe all types of illustrative matter ... unless other particular types in the work are considered important enough to be specifically designated.[8]

The size of a book should be omitted from the collation in simplified cataloging.

Notes can be added to supply additional information thought necessary to complete the bibliographic description of a title. If a title is part of a series, this note is placed in parentheses after the collation (see Figure 27).

Normally, the only note to be used in simplified cataloging is that for a series. However, if desired, other notes can be added below the collation (or series note, if any) to supply information considered essential for the complete identification of a title; for example:

First pub. in London in 1968 under title: The first American.

Contents. --The hairy ape, By Eugene O' Neill. --The glass menagerie, by Tennessee Williams. --Who's afraid of Virginia Woolf? by Albert Albee. --etc.

Bibliography: pp. 210-225

Subject Cataloging. --Subject cataloging is defined as "that phase of the process of cataloging which concerns itself with the subject matter of books ... and the determination of subject headings."[9] A subject heading is a word or group of words which indicate the subject dealt with in a book or other material.

The main function of a subject heading is to provide a heading or entry in the index or catalog of the library's collection or collections under which all books or other materials on the same subject may be listed.

As a general rule, a title should be assigned the most specific subject heading possible; that is, the heading which will most accurately describe the subject covered by the work. The subject heading must be narrow in order to express the contents of a title sharply and accurately, not vaguely and loosely. [10]

For example, a title written exclusively about canaries should be assigned the subject heading "Canaries," not the broader term "Cage Birds," which includes other birds besides canaries; or a title exclusively about wheat should be assigned the subject heading "Wheat," not the broader term "Grain," which includes other grains besides wheat. If a broad subject heading is required to describe the subject completely, then a specific heading included within the broader term should not be assigned also.

The number of subject headings to assign to a title will depend upon the number of subjects which it covers. Most titles deal with one or two subjects only and will require only one or two subject headings; but others, written about several aspects of a subject or about two or more subjects, might require more than two headings.

If several aspects of a subject are covered in a title, a broad subject heading normally will describe all aspects; if two or more distinct subjects are covered, a subject heading for each will be necessary. Only occasionally will a title require more than two or three headings in a small library.

Sources of Classification and Cataloging Information

Sources of Classification Information. --Several sources of information can be used in assigning classification numbers to materials. The most important source is

the material itself.   The title page, preface, foreword,
introduction, table of contents, and excerpts from the text
should be read or scanned to determine the classification
number.

The classification scheme chosen by the library will
be a prime source of information for classifying materials.

The introduction to the Dewey Decimal Classification
scheme includes instructions for its use and short summaries
of the classes and subdivisions of the classification system.
An important feature of the scheme is its relative index,
which indicates:

> ... under each entry the different senses in
> which the term is used and the diverse aspects
> of the subject with their appropriate places in
> the classification scheme. [11]

The Library of Congress Classification scheme consists of many tables in many volumes, each containing a
short summary of the class before the detailed divisions
and subdivisions are displayed.   There is a separate index
for each main class number but no general index for the
total system of classification.   Instructions for using the
system are sketchy and uncoordinated, since many different
subject specialists have aided in the preparation and constant
revision of the system through the years.

The list of subject headings used by the library is a
good source of information for assigning classification numbers to materials.

Dewey Decimal Classification numbers are suggested
for each subject heading in Sears List of Subject Headings,
and Library of Congress Classification numbers are suggested for most headings in the Subject Headings Used in the
Dictionary Catalogs of the Library of Congress.   These

numbers are included only as a guide for possible use and
should not be assigned without first checking the classification scheme itself and the library's own shelf list for consistency.

If used by the library, printed catalog cards have
suggested classification numbers on the lower part of each
card or already printed at the top ready for use. These
numbers also should be checked in the classification scheme
and in the library's shelf list for consistency.

H. W. Wilson's Standard Catalog Series (Children's
Catalog, Junior High School Library Catalog, Senior High
School Catalog, Fiction Catalog, and Public Library Catalog),
as well as the Booklist and Subscription Books Bulletin, the
Publishers' Weekly, the American Book Publishing Record,
the National Union Catalog, and even the proofslips sold
by the Library of Congress include classification numbers
for the materials listed. These are very useful aids when
printed cards are not available or when card sets must be
prepared locally in the library.

Sources of Cataloging Information. --If printed cards
are used, complete descriptive and subject cataloging information will be available automatically on these cards.

A primary source of information for cataloging is
the material itself. All parts of a title--its cover, title
page, introductory pages, table of contents, the text of
the book, and so on--will be sources of information for
cataloging. Although the title or subtitle of a book or
other material often will give an indication of the subject
or subjects covered by its contents, this is not to be relied
on, since the title or subtitle may often be misleading.

For most of the materials that will be acquired by a small library, complete information needed for cataloging can be located in the H. W. Wilson's Standard Catalog Series, the Booklist and Subscription Books Bulletin, the Publishers' Weekly, the American Book Publishing Record, the National Union Catalog, or the proofslips sold by the Library of Congress.

A primary source of information for subject headings will be, of course, the subject heading list adopted by the library. The most frequently-used list of subject headings for small libraries (particularly school and public) is the latest edition of Sears List of Subject Headings. Terms in this list are simple and generally not technical in nature. The subject headings suggested for use on the H. W. Wilson printed cards are taken from this list.

The Subject Headings Used in the Dictionary Catalogs of the Library of Congress is a more complete list used by some medium-sized public libraries and by most college libraries. Terms in this list are specific, technical, and often complex. The subject headings suggested for use on the Library of Congress printed cards, in the National Union Catalog, the Publishers' Weekly, the American Book Publishing Record, the proofslips from the Library of Congress, and several other aids, are taken from this list.

Consistency in Classification and Cataloging

Consistency in Classification. --In many cases, there will be a choice of more than one classification number which can be assigned to a title. Efforts should be made to keep all titles on the same subject together on the shelves.

If some titles on a subject are assigned one classification number and other titles on the same subject are assigned another, the library user who goes directly to the
shelves for his material could overlook several titles for
which he is searching. Since the main purpose of a classification system is to group materials according to the subject with which they deal, inconsistency in assigning classification numbers tends to defeat this purpose.

Two chief methods of maintaining consistency in assigning classification numbers are:

1. To compare the classification number selected
   for a title with numbers used previously in
   the card catalog for the same and similar
   subjects;

2. To compare the classification number selected
   with the same number in the shelf list to see
   the nature of the titles previously classified
   with that same number.

Pencilled notes can be made in the classification
scheme itself as to decisions made pertaining to materials
which should or should not be placed in particular class
numbers. The maintenance of a policy manual for classification will also aid the cataloger to maintain consistency in
classification.

Consistency in Cataloging. --Maintaining consistency
in cataloging is essential to insure an efficient and service-
able index or catalog to the library's collection or collections. Following standardized methods of describing materials in a uniform sequence is important.

The two critical parts of cataloging in which consistency is essential are in the author statement and in the
subject headings.

In order that all books or other material by the same author might appear together in the card catalog, the same name or form of the name of an author should be used consistently. For example, for the author John David Doe, one catalog record should not be "Doe, John D. ," another "Doe, J. David," and another, "Doe, J. D."

Once the form of a particular name has been selected or "established," that form should be used consistently for all titles written by the same author which are added thereafter to the library's collection or collections. The card catalog should be consulted each time to determine if another title written by the same author has been cataloged previously.

When the form of an author's name is first selected or established, a "see" cross reference should be made if it is felt that a catalog user might search in the card catalog for any other form than the one chosen for entry. For example, a catalog user can be referred from Mrs. Stanley Marshall Rinehart (which is not used as the author's name) to Mary Roberts Rinehart (which is used as the author's name); from the pseudonym "Mark Twain" to the real name, "Samuel Langhorne Clemens."

Consistency in assigning subject headings to books or other materials is necessary to maintain all subject headings pertaining to the same subjects together in the card catalog. Unless they are together, a library user searching for books on a given subject might fail to find relevant books because they were listed under a synonym or variation of the proper heading.

The obvious method of maintaining consistency in assigning subject headings is to use the same subject heading

for all books or other materials written on the same subject that are added to the library's collection or collections.
A pencilled check mark should be placed beside each heading
or cross reference in the subject heading list when a heading
is first assigned to an item in the library. The check mark
will indicate that the particular heading or reference has
been authorized for use in the library's card catalog.

Sometimes it is necessary to use a heading that is
not found in the subject heading list. In this case, the
heading should be written in the margin of the page and a
line drawn, if necessary, to indicate its alphabetical location. Akers' Simple Library Cataloging can be consulted
for additional information on preparing subject authority
files.

When a subject heading is first assigned to a title,
all necessary cross references after the "x" under that
heading should be made. For example, a catalog user
can be referred from the spelling, "Hindoos," to the spelling, "Hindus"; from the term, "fuel oil," to the term,
"oil burners," etc.

"See also" cross references also can be prepared.
For example, a catalog user can be referred from "flowers"
to "wild flowers," where additional information may be found.

The Card Catalog

The library's card catalog is "a catalog in which
entries are on separate cards arranged in a definite order
in drawers."[12]

This catalog has two main functions:

    1.   To indicate what books and other materials
        (such as pamphlets, periodicals, maps,
        records, etc.) a library owns;

2. To indicate where these materials are located
in the library.

Since library users may not know the exact location
on the shelves of a book or other material for which they
are searching, its author or title, or in some cases, even
the subject under which an item is located, the card catalog
is designed specifically to answer four questions:

1. "Does the library have a book or other material by a given author?"

2. "Does the library have a book or other material with a given title?"

3. "Does the library have a book or other material on a given subject?"

4. "What is the location of a particular book or
other material in the library?"

Composition of the Card Catalog. --The card catalog
is composed of several types of cards, the most common
being author, title, subject, reference, and guide cards.

A card with the name of an author on the top line
is known as an author card (see Figure 28).

A card with the title of a book or other material
above the author line is known as a title card (see Figure
29).

A card with a subject heading above the author line
is known as a subject card (see Figure 30).

Reference cards are of several types, the most
common being "see" cross references, "see also" cross
references, and general references.

A "see" cross reference card refers a catalog user
from a name or subject not used as a heading in the
catalog to a name or subject which is used as a heading
(see Figure 31). Care should be taken that there are

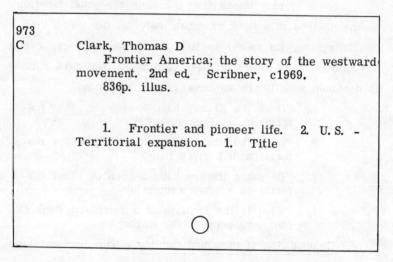

Figure 28. --An author card

973   Frontier America
C   Clark, Thomas D
                Frontier America; the story of the westward
         movement. 2nd ed.   Scriber, c1969.
                836p. illus.

Figure 29. --A title card

FRONTIER AND PIONEER LIFE

973
C   Clark, Thomas D
            Frontier America; the story of the west-
       ward movement.   2nd ed. Scribner, c1969.
       836p. illus.

○

Figure 30. --A subject card

Twain, Mark, pseud.

    See

Clemens, Samuel Langhorne

○

Figure 31. --A "see" cross reference card

Nibroc, Jon

See Also

Nibrok, John Bristow

Figure 32. --A "see also" cross reference card

BIOGRAPHY

The above heading is used for very general works;
that is, works about the writing of biography or
collections of biography not limited to any special
class of persons or to any locality.

For biography of a special class of persons, see the
name of that class, as SCIENTISTS - BIOGRAPHY;
for the biography of an individual, see the name of
that individual, as COLERIDGE, SAMUEL TAYLOR.

Figure 33. --A general reference card

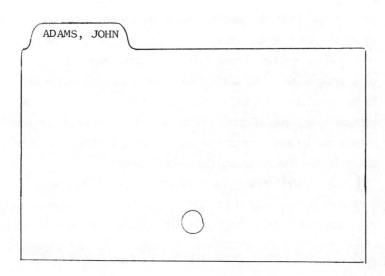

Figure 34. --A location guide card

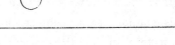

HOW TO USE THIS CATALOG

Cards are filed in this catalog under author, title, and subject, arranged alphabetically as the words in a dictionary.

The classification number is indicated in the upper left-hand side of each card; this number corresponds to the numbers on the spines of the books on the shelves, which are arranged numerically by the classification number, except for fiction and biography, which are arranged by author and biographee, respectively.

ASK THE LIBRARIAN IF YOU NEED HELP

Figure 35. --An instruction guide card

actually cards in the catalog under the author or subject to
which the user is guided.

A "see also" cross reference card refers a catalog
user from a name or subject to other names or subjects
in the catalog under which additional or allied information
may be found (see Figure 32). "See also" cross references
should not be inserted in the card catalog unless there are
cards in the file to which the user is guided.

A general reference card is a "blanket reference in
a catalog to the kind of heading under which [a catalog user]
may expect to find entries for material on certain subjects
or entries for particular kinds of names. "[13] (See Figure
33).

Guide cards also are of several types, the most
common being location and instruction guides.

A location guide has a projecting tab at the top,
with key letters or words on the tab, inserted at intervals
in the catalog to indicate arrangement and to aid the catalog
user in locating material (see Figure 34).

An instruction guide gives general information to
catalog users on using the catalog and in locating information in the file. These guides may be placed in the front
of each tray or at random intervals throughout the file
(see Figure 35).

Arrangement of Cards in the Card Catalog. --There
are several methods of arranging cards in a card catalog.
The method most often used in small libraries is to file
all cards (author, title, subject, reference, and guide
cards) together in one alphabetical sequence; this is referred to as a "dictionary catalog. "

However, the catalog can be divided into separate

author, title, and subject catalogs, with an alphabetical arrangement of the cards within each. Another common division is to arrange all author and title cards alphabetically
together in one catalog and all subject cards alphabetically
in another file.

If possible, cards should be divided among trays at
the ends of letters of the alphabet. However, if a decision
must be made whether to place half of the cards filed under
(for example) "S" in one tray and the balance in the next
tray, natural division points should be selected. For example, "Sa to Sm" in one tray and "Sn to Sz" in the next;
or, "Sa to Sm," "Sn to Sq," and "Sr to Sz," in case the
cards must be divided among three trays.

Tray labels serve two purposes: to indicate what
cards are filed in each tray and to keep trays in order
in a cabinet. The alphabet should be covered by the
labels, with no gaps; that is, one tray should not be labelled
"Aa to At" and the next "Ba to Bz," thereby omitting "Au
to Az."

Information on labels should be printed in large type
for legibility, with a piece of clear plastic over each label
to keep the print or ink from being soiled and smeared.
Each tray or label should be numbered to keep the trays
in order.

When possible, trays of catalog cards should not be
kept over two-thirds full; this will allow for future expansion
of the files without frequent shifting of cards from one tray
to another and constant preparation of new labels.

Sorting and Pre-Arranging Cards for Filing. --Before
newly-prepared cards are filed into the card catalog, they
should be sorted and pre-arranged into proper sequence

according to the filing rules adopted by the library (see suggested rules below) for easier merging into the trays of old cards. If a divided catalog is maintained, then separate files of new cards to be filed for each division of the catalog should be sorted and pre-arranged.

Filing Cards. --New catalog cards are merged with those already in the catalog or catalogs according to the filing rules adopted by the library.

Cards should first be filed into the trays without removing the locking rods. When all new cards are in place, each should be checked for filing accuracy (preferably by someone other than the person who filed them preliminarily). After this "revision" of filing and the correction of any errors found, the rods are pulled from the trays, the cards are dropped into place, and the rods are re-locked into position.

Most of the following rules suggested for use in a small library are based on those in Douglas' Teacher-Librarian's Handbook; rules 15 and 16 are based partly on those found in Akers' Simple Library Cataloging and the A. L. A. Rules for Filing Catalog Cards. Additional rules and a further explanation of the rules given here may be found in the aids mentioned above, particularly in Akers' Simple Library Cataloging.

1. Arrange all cards in straight alphabetical order except as noted below.

2. Arrange all cards by the first word on the top line of a card disregarding initial articles. Follow letter by letter to the end of a word and then word by word. Every word, including articles (except initial articles) and prepositions is to be regarded; for example:

Book
Book collecting
Book of famous ships
Book scorpion
Bookbinding
Books
Books and reading
Books that count
Booksellers and bookselling

When a name is used as an author, as a subject, and as a title, the name as author is filed first, then as subject, then as a title; for example:

Washington, George (as an author)
WASHINGTON, GEORGE (As a subject)
Washington, the city of light (as a title)

3. Arrange abbreviations as if spelled in full; for example:

"Dr. " as if spelled "doctor"
"Mr. " as if spelled "mister"
"Mrs. " as if spelled "mistress"
"M'" and "Mc" as if spelled "Mac"
"St. , " "Ste. " as if spelled "saint, " "sainte"

4. Elisions beginning with "D, " "L, " "O" are arranged as printed, disregarding the apostrophe; for example:

D'Angelo
L'Aiglon
O'Brien

Contractions are filed similarly; for example:

Who killed Cock Robin?
Who'd be king?
Who's who

5. Arrange compound words, both for persons and places, as separate words; for example:

Saint Gaudens, Augustus
St. Louis, Mo.
Saint Thomas College

6. Arrange personal and place names compounded
   with prefixes as one word; for example:

   La Farge
   Lafayette
   La Fontaine

   Van Bibber
   Vanbrugh
   Van Buren

7. Arrange hyphenated words as if separate words,
   disregarding the hyphen; for example:

   Happy home
   Happy-thought Hall
   Happy thoughts

   File as one word hyphenated words compounded
   with a prefix such as "anti," "co," "pre,"
   etc.; for example:

   Coe
   Co-educational
   Coerne

8. Disregard prefix titles such as "Mrs.," "Sir,"
   "Gen.," "Capt.," etc., in personal names except to distinguish between persons with the
   same name; for example:

   Scott, Sir Walter
   Scott, Walter
   Scott, Sir Yancey
   Scott, Yancey James

9. Figures in titles of books are alphabetized as
   if the words were spelled in full. They are
   not filed in numerical order; for example:

19th century [i. e., "nineteenth century"]
   literature
   Ninety-three palms
100 [i. e., "one hundred"] days to war

10. The apostrophe in the possessive case is dis-
regarded; for example:

   Boys' and girls' book
   Boys' king arthur
   Boy's will

11. Arrange the subdivisions of a subject heading
alphabetically, disregarding punctuation; for
example:

   ART, ANCIENT
   ART, FRENCH
   ART - HISTORY
   ART, ITALIAN

Exception: Under history of a country, subdivisions are arranged chronologically. Subject subdivisions precede period subdivisions.
If in doubt, use Sears List of Subject Headings
as a guide; for example:

   U. S. - HISTORY
   U. S. - HISTORY - DISCOVERY AND EX-
     PLORATION
   U. S. - HISTORY - COLONIAL PERIOD
   U. S. - HISTORY - REVOLUTION AND CON-
     FEDERATION
   U. S. - HISTORY - WAR OF 1812
   U. S. - HISTORY - CIVIL WAR
   U. S. - HISTORY - WAR OF 1898

12. Arrange subdivisions of a place alphabetically,
disregarding parentheses; for example:

   NORTH CAROLINA (STATE)
   NORTH CAROLINA (STATE) - HISTORY
   NORTH CAROLINA (STATE). HISTORICAL
     COMMISSION
   North Carolina State Farmers' Association

13. If two or more cards under an author's name
bear the same title, arrange by edition,
filing the most recent edition first; for example:

> 5th ed.
> 3rd ed.
> 1st ed.

14. Arrange publications of a government department together and then alphabetize by title;
for example:

> North Carolina. Dept. of Public Instruction.
>   Public Schools
> North Carolina. Dept. of Public Instruction.
>   School Library Handbook

15. Arrange Bible entries as follows:

> (a) Whole Bible
>   (1) As author
>   (2) As subject
> (b) New Testament, whole
>   (1) As author
>   (2) As subject
> (c) New Testament, individual books, alpha-
>   betically arranged
>   (1) As author
>   (2) As subject
> (d) Old Testament, whole
>   (1) As author
>   (2) As subject
> (e) Old Testament, individual books, alpha-
>   betically arranged
> (f) Bible as the first word of a title

16. Arrange Shakespeare entries as follows:

> (a) Works by
>   (1) Collected works (partial or com-
>   plete) in one alphabet
>   (2) Individual works by Shakespeare
>   in one alphabet, arranged by name
>   of play, using the short title (for
>   example, Hamlet, not Tragedy of

Hamlet). When the title of a
work is used as a subject heading, this is filed after the work
as a title

(b) Works about

Correcting Files for Withdrawn Materials. --Three
common reasons for removing records for books or other
materials from the library's files are:

1. If an item has been lost and paid for by a
    library user;

2. If an item is being discarded by the library;

3. If an item has been missing in two consecutive
    inventories of the collection or collections.

If the book or other material being withdrawn is one
of two or more copies, the catalog cards should not be dis-
turbed, as there is at least one other copy of the item in
the library's collection or collections.

If the book or other material being withdrawn is the
last copy and is not to be replaced, then the complete set
of cards (author, title, subject) for the item should be
withdrawn from the card catalog. If it is certain that the
book or other material is to be replaced soon with a new
copy, its catalog cards may be left in the files.

As a "lost" item often is "found" mysteriously at a
later date, catalog cards may be pulled from the file,
clipped together, and filed by author in a "withdrawn cards"
file in the technical services department for possible future
use or discarding. If an item is withdrawn because it is
not wanted, then its cards need not be kept but may be
discarded at the time the material is withdrawn, providing
it was the last copy in the collection or collections.

The Shelf List

The shelf list is a "record of the books and other materials in a library arranged in the order in which they stand on the shelves. "[14] This record, though not generally used by the public, is indispensable for the staff of the technical services department.

Functions of the Shelf List. --The shelf list has a number of functions in a library, the most important being:

1. To serve as a classified record of holdings;
2. To serve as an aid to classification;
3. To serve as a substitute for an accession record;
4. To serve as an aid in taking inventory.

Because its cards are arranged by classification number, or according to the arrangement of the books and other materials on the shelves, the shelf list serves as a classified record of the holdings of a library. Margaret Mann explains this in the following manner:

> [The shelf list] is the classification scheme filled in with book titles. The scheme is no longer a skeleton; the pigeon holes into which the books fit are occupied, and there is before the classifier, in card form, a workable and logical display of the titles in the library. [15]

Through an examination of the shelf list, one can see at a glance what books have been assigned a given classification number and what classification numbers have not been used. This aids the librarian to maintain consistency in assigning classification numbers to items on the same subject and indicates the extent to which classification numbers have been divided and subdivided.

The shelf list can serve as a substitute for an accession book. Information usually kept in an accession

Really? An 1972?

book, such as date of receipt, source, and cost of each copy of an item, can be placed on a shelf list card. This information is used to ascertain the cost when an item has been lost and must be replaced and to determine when and from whom an item was purchased.

Because it is a record of books and other materials arranged in the order in which they stand on the shelves, the shelf list is an indispensable tool in taking inventory of the library's collection or collections.

Composition of the Shelf List. --The shelf list contains cards which are exact duplicates of the author card or duplicates minus the notes and tracings.

In addition, each shelf list card should have recorded on it the "business information" for an item, including copy or accession numbers, the date each copy was received in the library, the source of each (such as the name of the vendor, donor, etc.), and the price paid for each copy.

Arrangement of Cards in the Shelf List. --The shelf list should be divided into several parts, the exact number depending on the type of library. The most common parts of a shelf list are adult nonfiction, adult fiction, young adult nonfiction, young adult fiction, juvenile nonfiction, juvenile fiction, easy books, biography, reference books, and short stories or short collections. Each part is maintained separately.

Shelf list cards for adult, young adult, and juvenile nonfiction titles and reference titles are arranged numerically (but separately) by classification number. Two or more cards with the same classification number are arranged alphabetically by author and two or more cards with the same classification number and the same author

are arranged alphabetically by title, ignoring initial articles
in the title such as "a, " "an, " "the. "

Shelf list cards for adult, young adult, and juvenile
titles, easy books, and short collections or stories are ar-
ranted alphabetically (but separately) by author.   Two or
more cards with the same author are sub-arranged alphabetically by title, again ignoring initial articles in the title.

Shelf list cards for biographies are commonly arranged alphabetically by the surnames of the persons written
about rather than by the author.   For this reason, the librarian might choose to have these names typed at the top
of their shelf list cards for ease of filing and use.

If possible, cards should be divided among trays at
the ends of broad classification numbers; for example, one
tray could hold cards for classification numbers "700"
through "750" and another, "751" through "799" (not "700"
through "749. 856" and 749. 857" through "799. ")

Tray labels serve to indicate what cards are filed
in each tray and to keep trays in order in a cabinet.   Information on the labels should be printed in large type for
legibility, with a piece of clear plastic placed over each
label to keep the print or ink from being soiled and
smeared.

The classification scheme or alphabet should be
covered by the labels, with no gaps; that is, one tray should
not be labelled "700" to "747" and the next, "750" to "799, "
thereby omitting "748" to "749. "

Guide cards should be inserted into the trays at intervals of approximately one inch to aid the user in locating
cards fast.   Preprinted shelf list guide cards are available

from most library supply houses or can be made easily
from blank guide cards.

When possible, trays of shelf list cards should not
be kept over two-thirds full; this will allow for future expansion of the files without the frequent shifting of cards
from one tray to another and will allow easy reference to
all the cards in the trays.

Sorting and Pre-Arranging Cards for Filing. --Before
newly-prepared cards are filed into the shelf list files,
they should be sorted and pre-arranged into proper sequence
(numerical for the classified parts and alphabetical for the
nonclassified parts) for easier merging into the trays of
old cards. Separate files are sorted and pre-arranged for
each part of the shelf list.

Filing Cards into the Shelf List. --New shelf list
cards are merged with those already in the shelf list.
Cards first are filed into the trays without removing the
locking rods. When all new cards are in place, each is
checked for filing accuracy (preferably by someone other
than the person who filed them preliminarily). After the
"revision" and location and correction of any filing errors,
the rods are pulled from the trays, the cards are dropped
into place, and the rods are re-locked into position.

are only filing errors checked for?

Correcting Files for Withdrawn Materials. --As for
the card catalog, three common reasons for removing the
records for a book or other material from the library's
files are:

1. If an item has been lost and paid for by a
   library user;

2. If an item is being discarded by the library;

3. If an item has been missing in two consecutive
   inventories of the collection or collections.

When a book or other material is withdrawn from the collection, its shelf list card is removed from the file and a line is drawn through the copy or accession number and other business information and "withdrawn, " "lost, " or "discarded" and the date are written after the entry. If there are other copies still in the collection, the card is then returned to its place in the shelf list file.

If the withdrawn book or other material was the only copy in the collection, then the shelf list card can remain out of the file and can be discarded or filed into an inactive or "dead" file. If it is certain that the item is to be replaced soon with a new copy, its shelf list card may be returned to the file.

Notes

1. American Library Association. Committee on Library Terminology, loc. cit. , p. 30.

2. Ibid. , p. 30.

3. Tauber, loc. cit. , p. 190.

4. American Library Association. Committee on Library Terminology, loc. cit. , p. 16.

5. Charles A. Cutter, Explanation of the Alphabetic-Order Marks (Three-Figure Tables) (Springfield: Huntting, n. d.), p. 4.

6. American Library Association. Committee on Library Terminology, loc. cit. , p. 24.

7. Ibid. , p. 45.

8. U. S. Library of Congress. Descriptive Cataloging Division, Rules for Descriptive Cataloging in the Library of Congress (Washington: Government Printing Office, 1949), p. 10-14.

9. American Library Association. Committee on Library
    Terminology, loc. cit., p. 136.

10. Mann, loc. cit., p. 143.

11. David Judson Haykins, Subject Headings: A Practical
    Guide (Washington: Government Printing Office,
    1951), p. 2.

12. American Library Association. Committee on Library
    Terminology, loc. cit., p. 43.

13. Ibid., p. 64.

14. Ibid., p. 126.

15. Mann, loc. cit., p. 95.

PREPARATION OF CATALOG AND SHELF LIST CARDS

Printed Cards

The use of printed cards in preparing catalog and shelf list cards for the library's collection or collections is recommended strongly. Not only can the time required to classify and catalog materials be minimized or eliminated but the staff time and the effort to prepare locally-produced cards can be reduced proportionately.

When printed cards are used, they should be ordered at the same time as the order for the books or other material is placed, to have the cards on hand when the material is received. Delays in processing the materials for use thus can be minimized or eliminated.

Some publishers or jobbers include sets of Library of Congress printed cards or their own printed cards with the purchase of books or other materials. These "free" sets of cards are either inserted inside the material, are placed separately in the shipping carton, or are mailed separately. While Wilson and Library of Congress printed cards are used most frequently by libraries, some vendors have their own printed cards for sale.

Wilson Printed Cards. -- Wilson cards are sold in sets only, with each set containing enough cards to catalog one title. The information on the cards is brief, with a minimum of punctuation. All cards in a set, except the shelf list card, contain an annotation or brief description

of the title, which is useful to a library user consulting
the card catalog in selecting materials for use.

Wilson cards are available only for selected titles
which have appeared or will appear in the Company's Standard Catalog Series (Children's Catalog, Junior High School
Library Catalog, Senior High School Library Catalog, Fiction Catalog, and Public Library Catalog). Complete check-
lists of sets of cards are available on a weekly, monthly,
or annual basis. The librarian should check to see that
printed cards are available before sending an order.

When sets of cards are ordered, the titles for which
cards are desired must be listed alphabetically by author
and title on an order form supplied by the H. W. Wilson
Company. An extra charge is made if books are not listed
in this manner.

Each set of Wilson cards costs $. 20. While checks
or coupons (which are sold in sheets of 25 for $5.00) must
accompany an order under $5.00, a library can be billed
for an order over this amount. Complete information about
proper ordering procedures, costs, and the order forms
can be obtained by writing to the H. W. Wilson Company,
950 University Avenue, Bronx, New York 10452.

As it is desirable that a record of the sets of cards
ordered be retained in the library, a carbon copy of each
order should be made and filed until all sets of cards requested have been supplied or until notification has been received that cards will not be available.

Sets of Wilson printed cards will be shipped to the
library in separate envelopes. As the sets are received,
they should be checked off the copy of the card order. If
the materials for which the cards have been ordered have

916.7 **Lineberry, William P**   ed.
           East Africa.   Wilson, H.W. 1968
           197p map (The Reference shelf v40, no.2)

           "This compilation . . . ᵣof articles and excerpts from books is intended asᵢ
           an over-all view of East Africa's progress and problems today." Preface
           Contents: The setting; The politics of independence; Economic problems
           and prospects; Race and society; East Africa's troubled neighbors; Bibliog-
           raphy

               1 Africa, East   ɪ Title   ɪɪ Series   916.7

           AFRICA, EAST
916.7 **Lineberry, William P**   ed.
           East Africa.   Wilson, H.W. 1968
           197p map (The Reference shelf v40, no.2)

           "This compilation . . . ᵣof articles and excerpts from books is intended asᵢ
           an over-all view of East Africa's progress and problems today." Preface
           Contents: The setting; The politics of independence; Economic problems
           and prospects; Race and society; East Africa's troubled neighbors; Bibliog-
           raphy

               1 Africa, East   ɪ Title   ɪɪ Series   916.7

           East Africa
916.7 **Lineberry, William P**   ed.
           East Africa.   Wilson, H.W. 1968
           197p map (The Reference shelf v40, no.2)

           "This compilation . . . ᵣof articles and excerpts from books is intended asᵢ
           an over-all view of East Africa's progress and problems today." Preface
           Contents: The setting; The politics of independence; Economic problems
           and prospects; Race and society; East Africa's troubled neighbors; Bibliog-
           raphy

               1 Africa, East   ɪ Title   ɪɪ Series   916.7

                              (W)   The H. W. Wilson Company

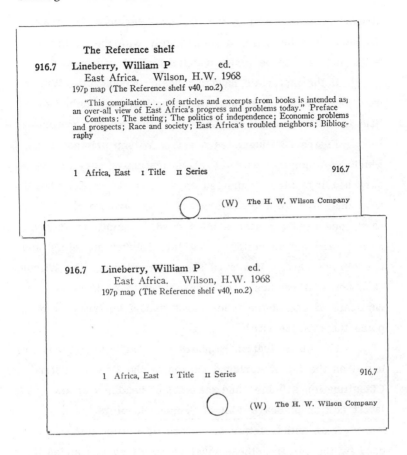

Figure 36. --A set of Wilson printed catalog cards

already been received in the technical services department, the cards can be matched immediately with the proper titles and all can be forwarded for further processing.

If the materials have not been received, the Wilson card sets should be arranged alphabetically by author or title in a file to await the arrival of the ordered materials.

Figure 36 illustrates a set of Wilson printed cards, which are complete with the classification number and necessary headings already printed on each card. A set should have one card for the author card, one card for the title card, one card for each subject card, possibly an "added entry" card for an editor, compiler, illustrator, etc., and a shelf list card. If a card should be missing, the Wilson Company will replace it or the set; but to avoid delays, a duplicate of one of the other cards should be typed to replace the missing card.

The classification numbers used on Wilson cards are based on the latest abridged edition of the Dewey Decimal Classification scheme, and the subject headings on the latest edition of Sears List of Subject Headings.

If an author letter or letters or Cutter numbers are used by the library, these must be prepared and added below the classification number on each printed card in order to complete each title's call number.

Before a book or other material with Wilson printed cards is processed, the cards should be compared with the title page and other parts of the item to make certain that the cards fit the title. The classification number should be checked in the shelf list to make certain that it is in agreement with the previous use of that number, or, if not previously used, that it is satisfactory for use in the library.

Subject headings on Wilson cards are listed at the
bottom of each card, preceded by Arabic numbers. Each
heading should be compared with headings in the Sears List
of Subject Headings and, if found there, should be used
without change. If a subject heading is not in the list and
a synonym is not found, then the heading suggested on the
printed card should be accepted and pencilled in the margin
of the subject heading list.

Occasionally, the librarian will feel that a subject
heading in addition to those assigned by the H. W. Wilson
Company is essential. In this case, it should be made,
using an extra printed card if available, or by typing a new
one.

Any information to be changed on Wilson printed
cards should be changed on each card of a set with a typewriter. If the print cannot be erased clearly, it should be
marked through with a straight ink line and the new information typed below, above, or beside the old.

If an additional card to a set is made, if the wording in a heading is changed, or if a card in a set is not
used but discarded, an indication of the change should be
made in the list of subject and other headings (the "tracings") at the bottom of the author card only. This list of
headings becomes the only means of locating the various
cards of a set when they are filed in different locations in
the card catalog and shelf list.

Library of Congress Cards. --One of the principal
features of Library of Congress printed cards is that
only one form of the card is sold: the author or "main
entry" card. All other cards (title, subject, shelf list,
etc.) must be prepared locally by adding headings or other
information to copies of this basic or "unit" card.

The Library of Congress, on its printed cards, attempts to describe a book more completely and in greater detail than does the Wilson Company on its cards. The author's name is given in full, with dates of birth and death and titles such as "dr. , " "viscount, " "president, " "capt. , " and so on. The title and subtitle, imprint, and collation are detailed enough to describe each title accurately and exhaustively; contents and/or other analytical descriptive notes take the place of the annotations found on Wilson cards.

Subject headings suggested on Library of Congress cards are those used in the main dictionary catalogs of the Library of Congress (and published in the Subject Headings Used in the Dictionary Catalogs of the Library of Congress). On cards printed after 1930, both Library of Congress and suggested unabridged Dewey Decimal Classification system numbers are given. Cards for some titles will have two Dewey numbers suggested, in which case the local library must choose the one best suited for its needs.

Beginning in 1967, suggested Dewey numbers have caret marks in them, indicating at which length the numbers may be modified or shortened for small- or medium-sized libraries.

Library of Congress printed cards are available for most titles published each year in the United States and for many published outside the country. Generally, if the Library of Congress acquires a title, Library of Congress printed cards will be available for sale to other libraries. These will be listed in the National Union Catalog, the Publishers' Weekly, the American Book Publishing Record, and several other sources.

The ordering of Library of Congress cards is more complex than for Wilson cards. Each set of Library of Congress cards must be ordered on a separate, special optical character recognition (OCR) order form furnished free by the Library of Congress; no orders listed on sheets will be accepted.

If a library uses a multiple-copy order form, one part of this set can be designed for ordering LC cards, but the specifications for forms other than those distributed by the Library of Congress are quite stringent and must be approved by that agency before orders for cards can be submitted. Figure 37 illustrates the latest order form adopted by the Library of Congress for ordering its printed cards.

Each library desiring to purchase Library of Congress printed cards should write to the Card Division, the Library of Congress, Washington, D. C. 10540, for the assignment of a subscriber number, a supply of order forms, and detailed instructions concerning procedures for preparing the order forms, submitting them, paying for the cards, and so on.

Library of Congress printed cards can be ordered either by Library of Congress card number or by author and title. The LC card number can be found on the back of the title page of all copyrighted materials published in the United States, in the National Union Catalog, in the Cumulative Book Index, the Publishers' Weekly, the American Book Publishing Record, and in many other bibliographic and reviewing aids.

The cost of the first copy of a card for any title is $.15; the cost of each additional copy of a card for the same title is $.04. A searching fee of $.40 is charged if

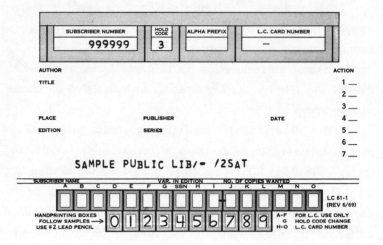

Figure 37.--The order form to be used to order
Library of Congress printed cards

cards are not ordered by its Library of Congress card number. If an order form is unreadable because it is not completed according to the Library of Congress' instructions, an extra $. 05 fee is charged.

Libraries can pay for cards by an advance deposit of money with the Library of Congress or upon receipt of a bill, according to the method that is most convenient to the individual library. Advance deposit is made by sending a sum of money to the Library of Congress before an order for cards is sent. The cost of each card order is deducted automatically from the deposit until the funds are depleted. An itemized statement is mailed monthly to the library.

A copy of each order form should be retained in the technical services department. If multiple-copy order forms are used, one part of the set can be inserted into a file indicating that LC cards have been ordered; or a carbon of each order form can be made on a scratch slip (not another LC order form) and these copies can be retained as a record of cards ordered. The part of the multiple-copy order form placed in the "on order" or "vendor on order" files can serve as a record that LC cards have been ordered, if desired.

Library of Congress cards will be shipped to a library with the original order form in front of each set of cards. If the materials for which the cards have been ordered have already been received in the technical services department, the cards can be matched immediately with the proper titles and all can be forwarded for further processing. If the materials have not been received, the LC card sets should be arranged alphabetically by author or title in a file to await the arrival of the ordered materials.

Figure 38 is an illustration of a Library of Congress card. The proper number of cards ordered by the library usually is indicated by a formula on the LC order form. The common formula is "2SAT, " which means:

> Send two cards, plus one card for each subject and added entry; send one additional card for the title entry, if it is not included in the added entries indicated on the card. This recommended formula will provide both a dictionary set and shelf list card. [1]

Before a title with Library of Congress printed cards is processed, the cards should be compared with the title page and other parts of the item to make certain that the cards fit the title. The suggested classification number should be checked in the shelf list to make certain that it is in agreement with the previous use of that number, or, if not previously used, that it is satisfactory for use in the files.

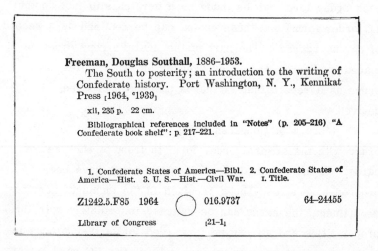

Figure 38. --A Library of Congress printed card

If the Dewey Decimal Classification system is used by the library, the class number suggested on the printed card should be checked in the shelf list and shortened if necessary by eliminating all parts of the number to the right of any caret mark in the suggested number. Some suggested numbers will have no caret mark (which means that the number should be used as it is), some will have only one, and others will have a maximum of two.

Subject headings listed at the bottom of LC cards are numbered. Each heading should be compared with headings in the list of Subject Headings Used in the Dictionary Catalogs of the Library of Congress and, if found there, may be used without change. If a subject heading is not found in the list and a synonym or cross reference is not found or the heading is not listed in one of the supplements to the list, then the heading suggested on the printed card should be accepted and pencilled in the margin of the subject heading list.

A large library is likely to make an entry card for all titles, subjects, editors, compilers, translators, etc., listed at the bottom of the Library of Congress cards. A small library should use few or none of these except the author, title, subject, and shelf list cards.

Any information to be changed on the printed cards should be changed on each card of the set with a typewriter. If the print cannot be erased clearly, it should be marked through with a straight ink line and the new information typed below, above, or beside the old.

If an additional card to a set is made, if the wording in a heading is changed, or if a card in a set is not used but discarded, then an indication of the change should be made in the list of subject and other headings (the "trac-ings") at the bottom of the author card only. This list of headings becomes the only means of locating the various cards of a set once they are filed in different locations in the card catalog and shelf list.

Other Printed Cards. --Within the past few years, a variety of printed cards in addition to those sold by the H. W. Wilson Company and the Library of Congress have been offered for sale by publishers and by firms selling completely cataloged, classified, and processed library ma-terials.

While there are variations in the type, style, and degree of cataloging and classification, all closely resemble the standardized format for catalog cards previously dis-cussed and as seen in Figures 28, 36, and 38.

The exact number of firms offering printed cards for sale to libraries is unknown. Representative samples of some of these printed cards are shown in Figure 39 (Library Journal cards), Figure 40 (Random House Pub-lishers cards), Figure 41 (Professional Library Service cards), and Figure 42 (Richard Abel cards).

Instructions for acquiring these cards can be obtained by contacting a representative of the particular firms. The use of these cards in the library will be similar to using Wilson and Library of Congress cards.

When using several types of printed cards in the same card catalog and shelf list, care should be taken that the authors' names, the classification numbers, and sub-ject headings particularly are compatible with each other. For example, subject headings taken from Sears List of Subject Headings should not be filed in the same card

catalog with those taken from the list of Subject Headings
Used in the Dictionary Catalogs of the Library of Congress,
unless alterations to some of the headings are made or unless many "see" and "see also" cards are made.

Locally-Produced Cards

If printed cards are not used or are not available,
catalog and shelf list cards for books or other materials
must be produced locally. This can be accomplished by
hand-typing each card of a set on card stock; by hand-typing
the author or "main entry" on a form or offset master and
photographically reproducing or offsetting enough cards for
a set; by hand-typing the author or "main entry" card on a
form or card and by reproducing by xerography or other
office copier enough cards for a set; or by several other
methods.

For all of these methods of producing sets of cards,
except when all cards are hand-typed, the sets must be
finished by manually typing such variable information as
subject headings, titles, etc. , on all "added entry" cards.

Preparation of Copy for Cards. --It is the responsibility of the cataloger to provide copy to the typist for preparing sets of cards. This copy can be in the form of a
typed author or main entry card on a "p-slip" or scratch
card or a photocopy of a printed or typed card. In any
case, any editorial work or typographical corrections should
have been made or indicated by the cataloger before the
copy is released to the typist. Figure 43 is edited copy
given to the typist by a cataloger for the production of a
locally-produced and, therefore, simplified set of catalog
cards.

598.1   **George, Jean Craighead.**
Geo   The moon of the alligators. Illus. by Adrina Zanazanian.
           Crowell ₍c1969₎
           40 p.   illus.   (The thirteen moons)

             A story about a female alligator living in the swamps of
           Florida's Everglades, explaining how the delicate balance of
           nature allows her to survive in the proper ecological niche.

                        1. Alligators.   I. Title.

                           ALLIGATORS.
598.1   **George, Jean Craighead.**
Geo   The moon of the alligators. Illus. by Adrina Zanazanian.
           Crowell ₍c1969₎
           40 p.   illus.   (The thirteen moons)

             A story about a female alligator living in the swamps of
           Florida's Everglades, explaining how the delicate balance of
           nature allows her to survive in the proper ecological niche.

                     The moon of the alligators.
598.1   **George, Jean Craighead.**
Geo   The moon of the alligators. Illus. by Adrina Zanazanian.
           Crowell ₍c1969₎
           40 p.   illus.   (The thirteen moons)

             A story about a female alligator living in the swamps of
           Florida's Everglades, explaining how the delicate balance of
           nature allows her to survive in the proper ecological niche.

598.1   **George, Jean Craighead.**
Geo   The moon of the alligators. Illus. by Adrina Zanazanian.
           Crowell ₍c1969₎
           40 p.   illus.   (The thirteen moons)

             A story about a female alligator living in the swamps of
           Florida's Everglades, explaining how the delicate balance of
           nature allows her to survive in the proper ecological niche.

                      1. Alligators.   I. Title.

             B 31-072   598.1
             LJ Cards © 1969   p — i

Figure 39. --A sample set of Library Journal printed cards

940.54 **Bliven, Bruce**
From Casablanca to Berlin: the war in North Africa and
Europe, 1942-1945. Illus. with photos.   Random House
©1965
180p illus photos maps index (Landmark books)

An account of Allied fighting in the European and Mediterranean
Theater of World War II, which traces the course of the conflict
from the first American landings in North Africa to the
unconditional surrender of Nazi Germany.

1 World War, 1939-1945—History I Title   940.54

WORLD WAR, 1939-1945—HISTORY

940.54 **Bliven, Bruce**
From Casablanca to Berlin: the war in North Africa and
Europe, 1942-1945. Illus. with photos.   Random House
©1965

From Casablanca to Berlin

940.54 **Bliven, Bruce**
From Casablanca to Berlin: the war in North Africa and
Europe, 1942-1945. Illus. with photos.   Random House
©1965
180p illus photos maps index (Landmark books)

An account of Allied fighting in the European and Mediterranean

940.54 **Bliven, Bruce**
From Casablanca to Berlin: the war in North Africa and
Europe, 1942-1945. Illus. with photos.   Random House
©1965
180p illus photos maps index (Landmark books)

1 World War, 1939-1945—History I Title   940.54

Random House
School & Library Service, Inc.
New York, N.Y. 10022
0708   Y412   1-6

Figure 40. --A sample set of Random House printed cards

QL   Filloux, Jean Claude, 1921–
785   The psychology of animals. Translated by
F5183   James J. Walling. New York, Walker [1963]

     148 p. illus. 21 cm. (Walker sun books, SB-19.
     Psychology and sociology)

    1. Psychology, Comparative. I. Title.

PSYCHOLOGY, COMPARATIVE

QL   Filloux, Jean Claude, 1921–
785   The psychology of animals. Translated by
F5183   James J. Walling. New York, Walker [1963]

     148 p. illus. 21 cm. (Walker sun books, SB-19.
     Psychology and sociology)

    1. Psychology, Comparative. I. Title.

The psychology of animals

QL   Filloux, Jean Claude, 1921–
785   The psychology of animals. Translated by
F5183   James J. Walling. New York, Walker [1963]

     148 p. illus. 21 cm. (Walker sun books, SB-19.
     Psychology and sociology)

    1. Psychology, Comparative. I. Title.

QL785. F5183   591.5   62-19509

Figure 41. --A sample set of Professional Library
Service printed cards

```
LC          Johnson, Charles Spurgeon, 1893—
2781
J6              The Negro college graduate, by
1969b        Charles S. Johnson.  New York,
             Negro Universities Press ᴌ1969ᴊ
             xvii, 399 p.  illus., 4 maps.
             24 cm.
```

```
            NEGROES — MORAL AND SOCIAL
              CONDITIONS
LC          Johnson, Charles Spurgeon, 1893—
2781
J6              The Negro college graduate, by
1969b        Charles S. Johnson.  New York,
             Negro Universities Press ᴌ1969ᴊ
             xvii, 399 p.  illus., 4 maps.
             24 cm.
```

```
            NEGRO UNIVERSITIES AND COLLEGES —
              ALUMNI
LC          Johnson, Charles Spurgeon, 1893—
2781
J6              The Negro college graduate, by
1969b        Charles S. Johnson.  New York,
             Negro Universities Press ᴌ1969ᴊ
             xvii, 399 p.  illus., 4 maps.
             24 cm.

             SBN 8371—1392—X
             Reprint of the 1938 ed.
             Bibliography: p. 378—384.
```

```
            The Negro college graduate.

LC          Johnson, Charles Spurgeon, 1893—
2781
J6              The Negro college graduate, by
1969b        Charles S. Johnson.  New York,
             Negro Universities Press ᴌ1969ᴊ
             xvii, 399 p.  illus., 4 maps.
             24 cm.

             SBN 8371—1392—X
             Reprint of the 1938 ed.
             Bibliography: p. 378—384.

             1. Negro universities and
             colleges—Alumni.  2. Negroes—Moral
             and social conditions.  I. Title.
LC2781.J6      1969b              331.7'1'0917496
                 SAMPLE               79—78768
                     69621255 B
```

Figure 42. --A sample set of Richard Abel
printed cards

973   Clark, Thomas David
CLA   Frontier America; the story of the
         westwrad movement. 2nd ed.   Scribner,
      →c1969.
             836p.   illus.

             1. Frontier and pioneer life.
         2. U. S. - Territorial expansion.
         I. Title.

Figure 43. --A sample of edited copy given to
the typist by a cataloger for the production of
a set of locally-produced catalog cards

The typist should know the format of the card set to be produced, including indentions, spacings, punctuation, etc. , and the number and type of cards to be produced.

Indentions and Margins. --The common indentions used when catalog cards are hand-typed are "first, " "second, " and "third" indentions. Although the spacings used in different libraries vary somewhat, the first indention usually begins on the ninth typewriter space from the left edge of the card; the second indention on the twelfth space; and the third indention on the fifteenth space.

The margin at the left of the card is from the edge to the ninth space (the first indention). The right margin is variable, depending on the amount of information to be placed on the card; but typing should not extend completely to the edge of the card. All lines should be single-spaced unless otherwise noted. Figure 44 indicates the indentions and margin spacings on a typed card.

Punctuation and Capitalization. --The following general rules for punctuation and capitalization in quotation marks are taken from the Catalog Rules of the American Library Association and the British Library Association. [2] Additional rules and examples were supplied by the author.

1. "The period is used (a) for abbreviations, but not after 1st, 2d, 3d, 4th, etc. ; (b) at the end of sentences or groups of items ... when they end with no other point ... ; (d) in contents (followed by a dash) to separate items"; for example:

   n. d.
   109p. illus.
   Contents. --Life of leisure. --Down the wind. --etc.

2. The comma is used between the main word

and the inverted parts of subjects and names,
after the place of publication and after the
publisher in the imprint, and elsewhere on
the title page; for example:

ART, AMERICAN
Jones, William Yeats
Random House, 1960

3. A dash is placed between a subject heading
and its subdivisions; for example:

U. S. - DESCRIPTION AND TRAVEL
AFRICA, WEST - ECONOMIC CONDITIONS

4. "Parentheses are used to signify inclusion,
as in the case of series notes ... "; for
example:

(Mainstream of America series)
(America first series, vol. 9)

5. A semi-colon is placed between the title and
the subtitle of a book; for example:

Window of the lost; a tale of woe
William Faulkner; his last days

In all doubtful cases, capitalization is avoided:

1. "Initial capital letters are to be used for
names or persons, personifications, places,
and bodies, for substitutes for proper names,
and for adjectives derived from these names;
for the first word of the title of a book; ...
for the second word of the title if the first
is an article. "

2. In most libraries, subject headings (including
sub-divisions) when typed at the top of subject cards, are typed entirely in black upper-
case letters (see Figure 45). Headings all in
black upper-case letters stand out on the
cards, are easily distinguished from titles
and other added entries, and do not require
a special typewriter ribbon; for example:

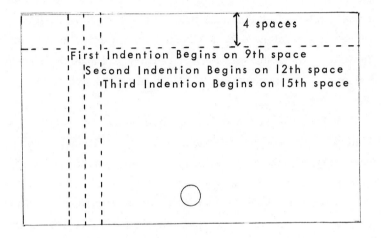

4 spaces

First Indention Begins on 9th space
Second Indention Begins on 12th space
Third Indention Begins on 15th space

Figure 44. --The indentions and margin
spacings on typed cards

BEETLES - U. S.
DEPARTMENT STORES - PERIODICALS
HARTSHORNE, CHARLES

<u>Preparation of Cards.</u> --In preparing an author card
or "main entry" card in simplified cataloging, the author's
name is placed on the fourth line down from the top of the
card, beginning at the first indention. The surname is
placed first, followed by a comma and any given names or
initials. Any additional lines necessary begin at the second
indention. No punctuation is placed after the author (see
Figure 45).

The title is placed on the line below the author, beginning at the second indention, with any additional lines
necessary beginning at the first indention. A period is
placed after the title (see Figure 45).

When the title is used in place of an author, a "hang-
ing indention" is used, in which case the title begins on the
author line at the first indention and all other lines begin at
the second indention.

The edition number, if any or other than the first,
is placed one space after the title, or after the names of
authors, editors, compilers, etc. , if included after the title;
a period is placed after the edition (see Figure 45).

The imprint, consisting of the publisher and the date
of publication in simplified cataloging, is placed two spaces
after the edition, or, if there is no edition number, two
spaces after the title. A comma is placed after the publisher and a period is placed after the date (see Figure 45).

The collation, consisting of the paging and an illustration statement, if any, is placed on the line below the
imprint, beginning at the second indention. The paging is

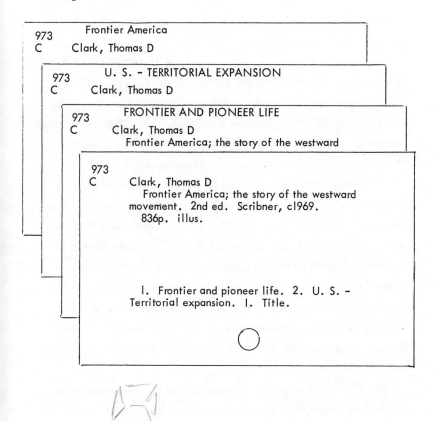

973   Frontier America
C   Clark, Thomas D

973   U. S. - TERRITORIAL EXPANSION
C   Clark, Thomas D

973   FRONTIER AND PIONEER LIFE
C   Clark, Thomas D
     Frontier America; the story of the westward

973
C   Clark, Thomas D
     Frontier America; the story of the westward
     movement. 2nd ed. Scribner, c1969.
     836p. illus.

     1. Frontier and pioneer life. 2. U. S. -
     Territorial expansion. I. Title.

Figure 45. --A set of hand-typed catalog cards

typed first, followed by the illustration statement, with two
spaces between the items (see Figure 45).

A series note, if any, is placed in parentheses two
spaces after the illustration statement (see Figure 45).
Other notes are placed on the second line below the collation, beginning at the second indention. Any additional lines
necessary begin at the first indention. If more than one note
is used, each is indented in the same manner.

The "tracings" (or list of subject headings and other
"added entries" to be made) are placed at the bottom of the
card just above the hole, on the author card only. In tracings, subject headings are typed first, beginning at the
second indention, and are numbered consecutively with
Arabic numbers; two spaces are left between each subject
heading. Tracings for other added entries, such as joint
authors, editors, illustrators, etc., are numbered with
Roman numerals and are typed after the subjects (see Figure 45).

The "call number" begins on the second typewriter
space from the left edge of the card. The author letter or
letters or Cutter numbers are typed on the same line as
the first line of the author statement (fourth line down from
the top of the card); the classification number or the special
symbol or number, if used, is typed on the line above the
author letter or letters or Cutter Numbers. A location
mark or other symbol, if used, is typed on the line above
the classification number (see Figure 45).

When hand-typed, added entry cards, such as subject cards, title cards, etc., are duplicates of the author
card described above, but without notes (except a series
note) or tracings.

The appropriate subject, title, etc. , is typed above the author line, beginning at the second indention. Additional lines, if necessary, begin at the third indention. The entire heading is centered between the top of the card and the author's name. Although the sub-division of a subject heading listed in the tracings may be abbreviated, it is spelled out completely when used as a heading on an added entry card (see Figure 45).

When hand-typed, the shelf list card also is a duplicate of the author card described above, again, without notes (except a series note) and tracings. The "business information" (date item received, source, and cost) is placed on the second line below the collation, beginning at the first indention, and with two spaces between each item. The copy or accession number of an item is placed in the left margin of the card opposite the business information for that copy, beginning in the second typewriter space from the edge of the card.

Both "see" and "see also" cross reference cards have the same format. The name or subject referred from is placed on the fourth line from the top of the card, beginning at the second indention. On the second line below this, beginning at the third indention, "see" or "see also" is placed.

The name or subject referred to is placed on the second line below "see" or "see also" beginning at the first indention. If additional lines are needed for any line, the next indention to the right is used (see Figure 46 and 47).

Notes

1. U. S. Library of Congress. Card Division, Instructions for Ordering LC Printed Cards (Washington: Library of Congress, n. d.), p. 6

2. American Library Association and the [British] Library Association, Catalog Rules: Author and Title Entries (American ed. Chicago: American Library Association, 1908), pp. 57-60

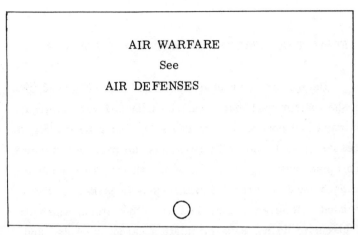

Figure 46. --A hand-typed "see" cross reference card

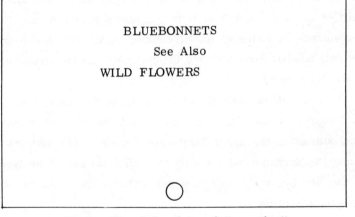

Figure 47. --A hand-typed "see also"
cross reference card

FINAL PREPARATION OF MATERIALS FOR USE

Before books or other materials can be placed on the shelves for use, each must be provided with a circulation card and pocket, a date-due slip, and a book plate (if necessary); each copy of a title must be property-stamped; each spine must be marked with the title's "call number"; and each must be provided with a plastic jacket, if these are used. Reference materials and other items which do not circulate do not have circulation cards, pockets, and date-due slips prepared or placed in them.

Preparation of Circulation Cards and Pockets

Circulation Cards. --Before a book or other item is loaned or checked out, it must be provided with a circulation card or a "book card," as it is commonly referred to. For convenience in matching the circulation cards with the books, the call number, the author's brief name, and the brief title of the book should be typed on this card.

The call number should be typed in the upper left-hand corner of the circulation card, and the copy or accession number in the upper right-hand corner. The author's name (the surname only usually is sufficient) should be typed on the line below the call number, and the brief title below the author's name.

There are many types of circulation cards available from most library supply houses. Most printing firms can prepare custom-made circulation cards if the library so

desires.   Figure 48 illustrates a commonly-used circulation
or book card with the information described above typed on
it.

Pockets. --The same information that is typed on the
circulation card can be typed on its pocket.   The call number should be typed in the upper left-hand corner of the
pocket, and the copy or accession number in the upper
right-hand corner.   The author's surname should be typed
on the line below the call number, and the brief title below
the author's name (see Figure 49).

As there are many types of circulation cards available, so there are many types of pockets.   If possible, the
library's name and address should be pre-printed on each
pocket.

Pasting

The book pocket can be pasted on the inside front or
back flyleaf of a book or other item, and the date-due slip
on the cover opposite the pocket.   The pocket should be
centered about one-half-inch from the bottom of the item,
and the date-due slip about one-half-inch from the top of
the item.

A fine film or several small dots of paste or glue
should be applied to the back of each pocket.   Pockets also
can be purchased with a special backing of dry adhesive.
When wet by a sponge or in a special machine designed for
the purpose, the pockets can be secured in the books.

If a plastic jacket is to be placed on the book, the
pocket should be pasted on the fly-leaf and the date-due
slip pasted on top of it and inserted down into the pocket
behind the circulation card.

973　　　　　　　　　　　　　　　c.l
C　　　Clark
　　　　Frontier America

DATE	ISSUED TO

B3　　　　　　　A.L.L. BOX 2442 ATLANTA,GA.

Figure 48. --A circulation or "book card" with the call
number, copy or accession number, author, and title
typed on it

If book plates are used for gift or memorial books, the donor's name, the honoree's name, or both should be typed on the plate. The plate can be pasted on the inside front cover of a book, but, depending upon the location of the pocket and the date-due slip and whether a plastic jacket is placed on the book, other locations can be used.

Marking Spines

The call number can be hand-lettered on the spine of a book or other item with pen and ink or with an electric lettering pen, though these methods are fast disappearing because of their costs, their slowness, and the lack of personnel capable of lettering neatly and properly. When the lettering has dried, if this method is used, a thin coat of shellac, lacquer, or plastic glue should be applied over the lettering to prevent the print from smearing or rubbing off.

The call number also can be typed on a pressure-sensitive label and the label placed on the spine of the book. Plastic glue brushed over the label will hold it in place and prevent smearing.

A recently-developed and satisfactory method of marking spines is the Se-Lin Labelling System developed by the Battelle Memorial Institute for the Library Technology Project. In this system, the call number is typed onto a strip of plastic tape. As typing is completed, another clear strip of tape is lowered over the first, thus protecting the letters from smearing. The labels are cut apart, the backing is peeled from the strips, and the labels are placed on the books or other materials. The labels are bonded to the spines by "ironing" them with a heating element.

If a plastic jacket is to be placed on a book, the call number should be typed on a pressure-sensitive label

973
C   Clark   c. l
         Frontier America

		DATE DUE		

Figure 49. --A pocket with the call number, copy or
accession number, author, and title typed on it

and the label placed on the dust jacket of the book; no plastic glue or lacquer should be brushed over the label, because the plastic jacket will hold the label in place and pro-
tect it from smearing.

Call numbers of books should be placed on all items
as nearly as possible at the same height from the bottom
page of the spines, though no measuring should be done.

Placing Plastic Jackets on Books

Placing plastic jackets on books requires an organization of the arrangement of the flow of books into the
process, the arrangement of the supplies, and some practice. The exact procedures will depend upon the type of
jacket used. An excellent description, with illustrations,
of placing plastic jackets on books can be found in Dennis'
Simplifying Work in Small Public Libraries. [1]

Jackets should be placed neatly and snugly over the
dust jackets and secured to the inside covers of the book.
If tape is used to secure the jackets, a strong, nonbleeding,
nondrying tape should be used; cellophane tape should not be
used under any circumstances. Some jackets have self-
adhesive strips that only require a protective covering to
be removed before the corners can be fastened to the inside covers of the book.

Property Stamping

A library's stamp of ownership, composed of the
name and location of the library, should be stamped in
each book or other item, the exact location varying with
the practice of the particular library. All impressions of
the rubber stamp should be neat and legible.

A stamp on the inside front cover, at the bottom of
the title page or at the bottom of the page after the title

page will usually suffice. Many libraries also stamp books
on the three outside edges for easy visual identification of
the materials as the library's property without opening them.

"Revising" the Work

Before books or other materials are shelved or are
sent to their final destinations, each should be checked or
"revised" to make certain that all processing steps have
been completed satisfactorily. Pockets and circulation cards,
date-due slips, marks of identification, call numbers, and
plastic jackets should be in their proper places, and the
catalog cards and shelf list cards should have been prepared,
revised, and be ready for filing or already filed.

"Revising" catalog and shelf list cards means checking or proofreading all cards before they are forwarded for
filing in the files. One important reason for revising the
cards is to insure accuracy. Misspelled words or names
and transposed numbers must be corrected. All cards of
a set must have the same call number, the same form of
the author's name, the same punctuation, capitalization, etc.
The format of the card (margins, indentions, spacings, etc.)
should be correct and uniform.

A second reason for revising cards is to insure
completeness. Every set should be checked to determine
that all required cards have been made and that all necessary information is on each.

A third reason for revising cards is to insure neat-
ness. Any card not in a neat form should be retyped. A
black typewriter ribbon which produces clear, dark type
should be used, and the keys should be cleaned often. All
type should be straight on the cards, with no strike-overs
and no smudges or unsightly erasures. Call numbers

should not run into the authors' names.

Any book which has been shoddily processed should be pulled from the flow and sent back to the appropriate person or persons for correction and/or improvement.

Notes

1. Donald D. Dennis, Simplifying Work in Small Public Libraries (Philadelphia: Drexel Institute of Technology, 1965)

SPECIAL PROBLEMS IN TECHNICAL SERVICES WORK

Work Simplification

Patrons have been attempting to communicate to librarians for decades the fact that they want rapid and easy access to library materials. They do not care if the spines of books are labelled carefully in measured hand-lettering; or if the pocket is pasted in the front or in the back of the book, or even if it has one at all; or if the copyright date is enclosed in brackets on the catalog cards if not found on the back of the title page; or if two dots are placed meticulously beneath the authors' surnames on the title pages of books. They just want the material they need, and fast!

However slow librarians in general have been in accepting this concept, patrons' sophistication, rising costs, lack of adequate staff, the "publication explosion," and other mounting pressures are causing them to search for better, faster, and less expensive means of acquiring, cataloging and classifying and further processing materials for the user of the library.

Streamlining, modernizing, and simplifying technical services work reduces costs and processing delays and permits the use of fewer staff members. This entails imagination, careful planning, and constant evaluation and re-evaluation of all functions performed by the department. Each operation should be examined from several viewpoints:

1. Are the steps involved in performing an operation the most efficient that can be devised?

2. Are the steps of each operation accomplishing this purpose?

3. Are any steps of any operation duplicating the work of another person in the department?

4. Are the steps involved in an operation, or the operation itself, really necessary?

5. Is the right person performing each operation?

If the answer to any of the above is "no," then adjustments should be made immediately. Each staff member should be encouraged to discuss with the administrator better methods of performing his operations. The staff member often knows of short-cuts that could be incorporated into his operations and should be given a chance to explain or demonstrate them.

One of the best manuals written for the small public library on work simplification is Dennis' Simplifying Work in Small Public Libraries, cited previously. The concepts in this manual can be used in other types of libraries as well as in public libraries.

Re-cataloging and Re-classifying

A fashionable trend lately is for libraries of all sizes (even small libraries of all types) to convert from Dewey or other classification systems to the Library of Congress system. Their reasoning appears to be that, with the advent of automation, with the furthering of standardization of classification policies and procedures and the acceptance of the Library of Congress as the base of that standardization, and with the inability of

isn't DC standardized?

your just said DC nos. appear on cards!

most libraries to recruit, train, and retrain qualified personnel, it behooves them to take advantage of the work already performed by the Library of Congress and made
available in a variety of publications, bibliographies, and
on printed cards.

Even if a library is not changing its classification
scheme, a certain amount of re-cataloging and re-classifying must be done from time to time.   When a new edition
or an addendum to the classification scheme used by the
library is published or a new subject heading list is issued,
a certain amount of change must take place in the library.
For example, a subject assigned one number in an old
edition of the classification scheme might be moved to a
totally different number in a new edition.

The cataloger then must either remove all materials
in the library's collection or collections assigned to the old
number and change the call numbers on the materials on
their catalog cards, shelf list cards, and other files;
leave all previously-classified materials on the shelves
and in the card catalog and shelf list with the old classification number and assign all newly-acquired materials to
the new number; or assign all newly-acquired materials
the old classification number even though the new number
is recommended in all available bibliographies and on
printed cards.

When subject headings become obsolete and are
changed or dropped, the same type of decision by the
cataloger must be made: to change all records to reflect
the subject heading changes or to leave the records as
they are.

Usually, every technical services department has a

certain amount of material going through its normal flow of operations which has been sent back to the department by other departments for re-cataloging, re-classifying, or correction of errors not previously detected.

Centralized Processing

A logical conclusion drawn by many is that costs can be reduced for a library if its technical services work is consolidated with that of other libraries to avoid the duplication of work and to gain the benefits of lower unit costs due to a higher volume of work based on mass-production methods.

A good definition of centralized processing is:

> Centralized processing may be considered to be those steps whereby library materials for several independent libraries either by contract or informal agreement, are ordered, cataloged, and physically prepared for use for library patrons, these operations being performed in one location with billing, packing, and distribution to these same libraries. [1]

A library can gain some or all of these benefits, and perhaps others, if the centralized processing center is well-organized, well-managed, and efficient.

By paying another organization to perform some or all of its technical services work, a library can reduce the size of its work space and reduce the number of staff members in the technical services department.

There are four basic types of centralized processing centers:

1. A library system which consolidates its ordering, receiving, cataloging, classification, and further processing of library materials in a central location for a main unit and one or more branches (for example: any large public library system or a school system

with centralized processing for all its units.

2. A library unit which contracts with other governmentally-separate libraries to perform the ordering, receiving, cataloging, classification, and further processing of library materials.

3. A service center independent of any one library unit but established specifically by and for a group of governmentally-separate library units to perform the ordering, receiving, cataloging, classification, and further processing of library materials (for example: Eastern Shore Book Processing Center, Southwest Missouri Library Service).

4. A commercial firm which sells its processing services for a profit (for example: Alanar, Professional Library Service).

In utilizing a centralized processing center of any type, the library must often accept the standards and methods of cataloging, classification, and further processing set forth by the processing center. A library that utilizes the services of a center does not, however, have to relinquish its autonomy in materials selection, services to users, or other areas governed by local policies.

There are always likely to be some processing steps that a centralized processing center cannot or will not perform; for example: property stamping, accessioning, filing cards. These operations have to be performed locally in the individual library. All materials received from a centralized processing center should be swiftly checked and scanned for shoddy or incomplete work, but a complete audit of all the processing steps should not be made, or much of the advantage of utilizing a processing center will be lost. Allowing a centralized processing center to perform some or all of the library's technical services work demands faith on the part of the local library that the center is performing quality and accurate work.

Pre-Processing

Pre-processing of library materials is a controversial matter among some librarians; many claim that it is impossible to do well and economically, others claim that it can be done readily. The truth probably lies somewhere between these positions: a percentage of the materials acquired by the small- to medium-sized library can be almost completely pre-processed before they are received, some can be partially pre-processed, and a small percentage can have no pre-processing done before the materials are received.

Pre-processing refers to the preparation of catalog and shelf list cards, pockets, circulation or book cards, and spine labels after the materials are ordered but before they are received in the technical services department. The pre-processed items can be inserted into the book pocket and the pockets placed by title, by author, or by order number or date in a file to await the receipt of the items.

Once received, the materials must be compared with the catalog and shelf list cards, labels, etc., to make certain that the pre-processing was performed correctly.

By ordering printed cards at the same time as the materials are placed on order with vendors, a certain amount of pre-processing is accomplished, assuming that the correct printed cards will be received before the material arrives.

"LJ" (Library Journal) kits are a form of pre-
processing. A kit of completely-prepared catalog and
shelf list cards, book pockets, circulation cards, and spine
labels is shipped with the books or other materials. The
library must place the business information on the shelf
list card and occasionally (depending upon the type of material) must type the call numbers on the cards and pockets.
Several commercial firms offer this or similar services to
libraries.

Automation and Mechanization

Sharing the current limelight with the "new media"
in libraries is automation and mechanization.

Mechanization can be accomplished easily even in
the small library by installing electric typewriters, multi-
lith machines, electric pasting machines, electric paper
cutters, electric pencil sharpeners, and a variety of other
simple equipment.

But automation entails a large investment of time,
talent, and money--elements not often readily available in
the small library. Automation implies the use of an elec-
tronic computer system or at least a less sophisticated
unit record equipment system. These require the services
of specialized personnel such as systems analysts, pro-
grammers, operators, and the funds to pay for these plus
the equipment itself. However, by sharing the costs of
personnel and equipment with other libraries, other organizations, other departments of a city, college, or school,
automation may soon be possible even for the small library.

Notes

1. James R. Hunt, "The Historical Development of Processing Centers in the United States," Library Resources and Technical Services. 8:1, Winter, 1964, p. 54

BIBLIOGRAPHY

The following bibliography has been assembled for two purposes:

1. To suggest a list of basic references which should form the departmental library of a small technical services department for its day-to-day activities of acquiring and processing materials.

2. To suggest a list of basic references which should aid the technical services administrator and other staff members to gain more knowledge in performing their assigned functions.

It is by no means exhaustive: it is selective because the small- to medium-sized technical services department must be selective by necessity in its purchase of professional and bibliographic reference aids, at least in its initial organization. While the value of periodical articles is recognized, none are listed here.

All items listed currently are in-print at the prices indicated. An item with one asterisk beside its citation indicates that it is essential for first-purchase by the small library; two asterisks indicate that an item can be used by a small library if funds are available, but it should be for first purchase by the medium-sized library; three asterisks indicate that a title will be useful to both small- and medium-sized libraries but is not essential to their normal operations.

This bibliography is arranged by author under three

broad subject headings of bibliographic, searching, and
book selection aids; professional reading and development
aids; and miscellaneous reference aids.

Bibliographic, Searching, and Book Selection Aids

Forthcoming Books. New York: Bowker. $19. 95/annual
subscription.
A bi-monthly list of all new titles announced for publication
within the coming half-year, with an author and title index
only.

*Junior High School Library Catalog. "Standard Catalog
Series. " New York: Wilson, 1965. With four annual
cumulations: $20. 00.
A selection of approximately 3, 300 fiction and nonfiction
titles for grades 7-9, useful in book selection, cataloging
and classification, and reference work. It is arranged by
the abridged Dewey Decimal Classification system, with an
author, title, subject, and analytical index.

**National Union Catalog. Washington: U. S. Library of
Congress. $403/annual subscription, including monthly,
quarterly, and annual cumulations.
The most comprehensive bibliography of materials published in the United States and other parts of the world that
is issued in America. Though a separate subject index can
be purchased, the main part of the National Union Catalog
is by author only. Complete bibliographic information, including subject headings, Library of Congress Classification
numbers, and suggested Dewey Decimal Classification numbers (unabridged).

*Public Library Catalog. "Standard Catalog Series. " 5th
ed. New York: Wilson, 1968. With four annual supplements for 1969-72: $50. 00.
Formerly titled the Standard Catalog for Public Libraries,
this bibliographic aid is a classified list of over 11, 000
nonfiction titles (the supplement will contain an additional
3, 500 titles) useful in the public library for book selection,
cataloging and classification, and reference work.

*Publishers' Weekly. New York: Bowker. $16. 50/annual
subscription.

A weekly news journal of the publishing world, which includes a "Weekly Record" of new books, including complete cataloging and classification information. Arranged
alphabetically by author.

*Publishers' Trade List Annual.   New York: Bowker.
1969 in 4 volumes: $14. 00.
A collection of publishers' catalogs bound together in alphabetical order, useful as a guide to the past, current,
and future publications of the various publishers which are
still available for sale.

*American Book Publishing Record.   New York: Bowker.
$16. 75/annual subscription.
A monthly cumulation of all listings in the "Weekly Record"
section of the Publishers' Weekly.   Arranged by Dewey
Decimal Classification system numbers, with an author
and title and subject index.   Cumulated annually.

*Ayer's Directory, Newspapers, Magazines, and Trade
Publications.   New York: Ayer. $40. 00.
An annual directory of newspapers and periodicals, ar-
ranged by city within state, with a title index.

*Booklist and Subscription Books Bulletin.   Chicago: Am-
erican Library Association. $10. 00/annual subscription.
Arranged by the Dewey Decimal Classification system,
this semi-monthly (with some biennial cumulations) reviews
books and other materials of all types that are useful for
all types of libraries.   Has a special section on free and
inexpensive materials and government publications.

*Books in Print; An Author-Title Index to the Publishers'
Trade List Annual.   New York: Bowker. $22. 00/two
volumes.
An annual author and title index in two volumes to all
titles indicated as being in-print from all publishers listed
in the Publishers' Trade List Annual.   Includes, authors,
titles, editions, publishers, types of bindings, prices, etc.

*Children's Catalog.   "Standard Catalog Series. "   11th ed.
New York: Wilson, 1966, with four annual supplements,
1967-1970: $17. 00.
Titles listed for school and public libraries, arranged by
the abridged Dewey Decimal Classification Scheme, with
good indexes.

*Cumulative Book Index. New York: Wilson. Priced on a "service basis rate," which is based on a library's annual expenditure for English-language books. Write the publisher for a quotation.
This comprehensive bibliography lists books published anywhere in the English language (except government publications, music, and pamphlets), containing excellent author, title, and subject approaches to the items indexed. Published monthly (except August) with semi-annual and two-year cumulations.

*Fiction Catalog. "Standard Catalog Series." 7th ed. New York: Wilson, 1960. $9.00. Fiction Catalog, 1961-1965, with four annual supplements: $11.00.
The 7th edition lists over 4,000 titles of fiction for all types of libraries, useful for book selection, cataloging and classification, and reference work.

*Senior High School Library Catalog. "Standard Catalog Series." 9th ed. New York: Wilson, 1967. With five annual supplements: $20,00. With Catholic supplement: $25.00.
Formerly the Standard Catalog for High School Libraries, this is a selection, cataloging and classification, and reference aid for fiction and nonfiction titles recommended for students in grades 10-12, with approximately 4,200 titles. Arranged by the abridged Dewey Decimal Classification system, with an author, title, subject, and analytical index. Available also with a Catholic supplement.

*Subject Guide to Books in Print; an Index to the Publishers' Trade List Annual. New York: Bowker. $19.25. 2 volumes.
An annual listing by subject of all titles included in the Publishers' Trade List Annual, which in turn is indexed by author and title in Books in Print.

*Ulrich's International Periodicals Directory. 12th ed. New York: Bowker, 1967-68. $15/per volume.
A comprehensive listing of periodicals of all types and on all subjects, arranged by subject with a title index.

*Vertical File Index. New York: Wilson. $8.00/annual subscription.
A monthly (except August) catalog of pamphlets, leaflets, etc., of interest to all types of libraries, arranged by

subject with a title index. Includes names and addresses
of sources of materials and costs, if any.

Professional Reading and Development Aids

*Akers, Susan Grey. Simple Library Cataloging. 5th ed.
Metuchen: Scarecrow Press, 1969. $7.50.
A companion to Mann's Introduction to Cataloging and the
Classification of Books, oriented mainly to simplified
cataloging but covering all types of materials, with many
examples of sample catalog cards. Includes some common-
sense rules for filing cards in a dictionary catalog, based
on the A. L. A. Rules for Filing Catalog Cards.

*Carter, Mary Duncan, and Bonk, Wallace John. Building
Library Collections. 3rd ed. Metuchen: Scarecrow
Press, 1969. $7.50.
While this text concentrates on the methodology of selecting and organizing collections of all types of libraries,
there are excellent sections on weeding the collection,
censorship, selection and acquisition policies, and good
annotations of reference aids used in selection and in
acquisitions work.

***Casey, Robert S. , et al. Punched Cards: Their Applica-
tion to Science and Industry. 2nd ed. New York: Rein-
hold, 1958. $20.00.
Only one chapter will interest the librarian, but it is one
of the best overviews of the use of punched cards of all
types in libraries.

**Dunkin, Paul S. Cataloging U. S. A. Chicago: American
Library Association, 1969. $5.00.
A basic text on the theory of cataloging, dwelling mainly
on the "why" rather than on the "how" of cataloging.

**Gardiner, Jewel. Library Service in the Elementary
School. 2nd ed. Chicago: American Library Association,
1954. $3.50.
A general guide for providing library service in elementary
schools.

**Haines, Helen. Living with Books. 2nd ed. New York:
Columbia University Press, 1950. $7.50.
A somewhat outdated but still usable guide to selecting
books for all types of libraries, but with emphasis on
public libraries.

**Herdman, Margaret M. Classification: An Introductory
Manual. 2nd ed. Chicago: American Library Association,
1947. $11. 00.
A simplified study of classification systems, book numbers,
rules, etc.

*Ireland, Norma O. The Pamphlet File in School, College,
and Public Libraries. Boston: Faxon, 1954. $6. 25.
One of the only texts on handling the pamphlet file in libraries, including its organization and maintenance.

***Kimber, Richard T. Automation in Libraries. New York:
Pergamon Press, 1968. $6. 00.
An introduction to computers and automation in libraries
of all types, with discussions of applications of automation
in the different areas of libraries (particularly technical
services).

**Lowy, George. A Searcher's Manual. Hamden: Shoe
String Press, 1965. $4. 50.
A well-presented manual on the procedures of searching
and verifying information for requests for purchase by the
library.

***Lyle, Guy R. , et al. The Administration of the College
Library. 3rd ed. New York: Wilson, 1961. $8. 00.
A complete introduction to all aspects of college library
administration.

*Mann, Margaret. Introduction to Cataloging and the Classi-
fication of Books. 2nd ed. Chicago: American Library
Association, 1943. $4. 00.
An indispensible aid for the administrator, cataloger, and
classifier as a comprehensive source of information on the
organization, cataloging, and classification of library materials, including practical information on organizing and
simplifying the work. Can be used by small- and medium-
sized libraries alike.

*Osborn, Andrew. Serial Publications: Their Place and
Treatment in Libraries. Chicago: American Library
Association, 1955. $6. 00.
The standard text on handling all aspects of serials or
periodicals work.

*Piercy, Esther J. Commonsense Cataloging; A Manual for the Organization of Books and Other Materials in School and Small Public Libraries. New York: Wilson, 1965, $5. 00.
An excellent manual on current and simplified cataloging of library materials for school and public libraries, including practical step-by-step operations for beginners.

*Rufsvold, Margaret. Audio-Visual School Library Service; A Handbook for Librarians. Chicago: American Library Association, 1949. $2. 75.
While this text deals mainly with audio-visual aids in general, it is useful in technical services work.

*Sinclair, D. Administration of the Small Public Library. Chicago: American Library Association, 1965. $5. 00.
A good text on the administration of a small public library with a staff of under three professional librarians.

***Tauber, Maurice and Associates. Technical Services in Libraries: Acquisitions, Cataloging, Classification, Binding, Photographic Reproduction, and Circulation Operations. New York: Columbia University Press, 1953. $10. 00.
This important classic is aimed at large research libraries, but the principles discussed often can be scaled down to small libraries.

***Wasserman, Paul. Librarian and the Machine; Observations on the Applications of Machines in Administration of College and University Libraries. Detroit: Gale Research, 1965. $5. 75.
While this little volume is written about college and university libraries, many of the essays are applicable to all types of libraries contemplating automation.

***Wheeler, Joseph L. , and Goldhor, Herbert. Practical Administration of Public Libraries. New York: Harper, 1962, $8. 95.
A practical guide for administration and planning in libraries in cities with a population from 10, 000-500, 000.

***Wilson, Louis Round, and Tauber, Maurice F. The University Library: The Organization, Administration, and Function of Academic Libraries. 2nd ed. New York: Columbia University Press, 1956. $12. 50.

The basic principles of college and university library
administration which can aid the technical services librarian in gaining an insight into the role of the library
in the college and university environment and, therefore,
the role of the technical services department.

*Wofford, Azile. The School Library at Work; Acquisition,
Organization, Use and Maintenance of Materials in the
School Library. New York: Wilson, 1959. $5. 00.
A well-organized guide to acquisitions, processing, and
using materials in school libraries.

**Wulfekoetter, Gertrude. Acquisitions Work: Processes
Involved in Building Library Collections. Seattle: University of Washington Press, 1961. $6. 95.
While the arrangement of this text is somewhat disor-
ganized, it covers a wide range of acquisitions work and
should be on the shelf of every administrator of a
medium-sized technical services department. Also covers
the selection of materials.

Miscellaneous Reference Aids

*A. L. A. Rules for Filing Catalog Cards. 2nd ed.
Chicago: American Library Association, 1968. $6. 75.
The best guide available to the small- and medium-sized
library for filing cards in a dictionary card catalog.
Covers virtually all types of situations with numerous
examples and a good index. Available also in an
abridged edition.

*American Book Trade Directory. New York: Bowker.
$25. 00
A biennial directory of publishers of all types, book jobbers and distributors, search specialists, and bookstores
listed by state and city.

*American Library Association. Board of Personnel Ad-
ministration. Descriptive List of Professional and Non-
Professional Duties in Libraries. Chicago: American
Library Association, 1948. $1. 50
Though this pamphlet is somewhat outdated, it remains
the best guide for distinguishing between professional
and nonprofessional duties in all phases of library work,
including technical services.

**American Library Association. Committee on Library
Terminology. A. L. A. Glossary of Library Terms, With
a Selection of Terms in Related Fields. Chicago: American Library Association, 1943. $4. 00.
While out-of-date and lacking in coverage of technical
services work, this still must be considered one of the
best authorities for defining terms in library science.

*Anglo-American Cataloging Rules. North American text.
C. Sumner Spaulding, general editor. Chicago: American
Library Association, 1967. $8. 50.
Superseding the A. L. A. Catalog Rules for Author and
Title Entries, this is the authoritative text now for
cataloging all types of materials.

***Bowker Annual of Library and Book Trade Information.
14th ed. New York: Bowker, 1969. $11. 50.
An annual providing a wide range of general information
pertaining to libraries and publishers, including useful
statistics, standards, directories, and a library purchasing guide for supplies and equipment.

**Decimal Classification and Relative Index. 17th ed. New
York: Forest Press, 1965-67. 2 volumes. $30. 00/set.
A controversial revision of the unabridged Dewey Decimal
Classification scheme, with several important changes
over the 16th edition but with the upgrading of many areas
to keep pace with the rapidly-changing knowledge.

*Decimal Classification and Relative Index. 9th abridged
ed. New York: Forest Press. 1965. $10. 00.
Based on the revised 17th edition but intended for the
small- to medium-sized library.

**Reader's Advisor and Bookman's Manual; A Guide to the
Best in Print in Literature, Biographies, Dictionaries,
Encyclopedias, Etc. 11th ed. New York: Bowker,
1969. 2 volumes. $20. 35, vol. 1; $14. 50, vol. 2.
A standard and essential book selection aid for all li-
braries.

*Sears List of Subject Headings, ed. by Barbara M. West-
by. 9th ed. New York: Wilson, 1965. $8. 00.
The standard list of subject headings used by many small
libraries of all types. H. W. Wilson uses these subject
headings on their printed cards.

***U. S. Library of Congress. Descriptive Cataloging Division. Rules for Descriptive Cataloging in the Library of Congress (adopted by the American Library Association). Washington: U. S. Library of Congress, 1949. $2. 00.
A guide for the cataloger, with rules for descriptive cataloging, useful explanations of the rules, and many examples. While the small- to medium-sized library would not follow all of these rules, if Library of Congress printed cards are used, this text will explain the information found on the cards.

***U. S. Library of Congress. Processing Department. Filing Rules for the Dictionary Catalogs of the Library of Congress. Washington: U. S. Government Printing Office, 1956. $2. 25.
While the small- to medium-sized library would use the simplified rules recommended by the American Library Association, this book can be used as a supplement, especially when a large amount of cards accumulate under an author, title, or subject heading in the card catalog.

**U. S. Library of Congress. Subject Cataloging Division. Subject Headings Used in the Dictionary Catalogs of the Library of Congress. 7th ed. Washington: U. S. Library of Congress. 1966. $15. 00. Annual subscription for supplements: $2. 50.
The standard list of subject headings used by most medium and large libraries using Library of Congress printed cards.

*Winchell, Constance. Guide to Reference Books. 8th ed. Chicago: American Library Association, 1967. $15. 00.
A guide to the selection and use of reference books, with annotations for over 8, 000 reference titles.

***Wynar, Bohdan S. Library Acquisitions; A Classified Guide to the Literature and Reference Tools. "Library Science Text Series." Rochester: Libraries Unlimited, 1968. $7. 00.
A somewhat bewildering and unselective yet comprehensive bibliography of books and articles mostly on library acquisitions but also on technical services in general.